A QUICK GUIDE THROUGH THE BIBLE

Easily Grasp the Whole Bible and How to Interpret It

ROSS LYON

 LEHIGH PUBLISHERS
2740 Old Post Road
Schnecksville, PA 18078

References marked in bold are suggested readings in Scripture, as you follow this guide.

Quotations are in *italics* and Scripture quotations are in ***bold italics***.

When you see "John 3:16," it means the name of the book in the Bible, the chapter, and the verse.

Large margins are provided for personal notes.

Ross D. Lyon, D.Min., Ph.D., has also written *A Clear Guide to Genesis*, and *A Clear Guide to Revelation*.

TABLE OF CONTENTS

Old Testament

Chapter One...........................*page 6*
Why the Bible is a Miracle, pp. 5-6
How to Interpret the Bible, pp. 6-8
Types of Books in the Bible, p.10

Chapter Two...........................*page 11*
Genesis, the Foundation
Why God Allows Bad things, p.16
What Should We Know for Salvation, p. 23

Chapter Three...........................*page 29*
Exodus, Leviticus,
Numbers, Deuteronomy
10 Plagues, p. 32; 10 Commandments,p.34

Chapter Four...........................*page 34*
Joshua, Judges, Ruth

Chapter Five...................*page*.......... *47*
I & II Samuel, I & II Kings
I & II Chronicles
Monarchy VS. Theocracy, p.48
Old Testament World Wide Missions, p.51
Number of Good and Bad Kings, p.53

Chapter Six...........................*page 57*
Ezra, Nehemiah, Ezra
Divorce in the Old and New Testaments, p.58

Chapter Seven...........................*page 61*

Job, Psalms, Proverbs,
Ecclesiastes, Song of Songs
How to Interpret the Psalms, pp. 63-64

Chapter Eight.............................page 67
    Isaiah, Jeremiah,
    Lamentations, Ezekiel,
    Daniel
When the Prophets wrote, p. 67

Chapter Nine............................page 73
    Hosea, Joel, Amos,
    Obadiah, Jonah, Micah,
    Nahum, Habakkuk,
    Zephaniah, Haggai,
    Zechariah, Malachi
Evidence for Jonah and the Whale, p.76
The Major Covenants, p. 80

New Testament

Chapter Ten............................page 81
    Matthew, Mark, Luke,
    John, Acts
Water and Spirit Baptism in Acts, pp. 85-86
The Skeptic who Found Luke True, p.87

Chapter Eleven.......................page 88
    Romans

Chapter Twelve......................page 96
    I & II Corinthians, Galatians,
    Ephesians, Philippians

Chapter Thirteen..................page 109

Colossians, I & II Timothy
Titus
The Bible and Slavery, p. 110
'

Chapter Fourteen......................page 117
Hebrews, James,
I & II Peter, I,II,III John, Jude

Chapter Fifteen.......................page 125
Revelation
Three Views of the Millennium, p137.

CHAPTER ONE:
THE MIRACLE BOOK

The Bible was the first book ever to claim boldly it was the word of God! Not only that, it backed up its claims by its own writings.

The Bible was written through 1500 years by 39 authors of different times and cultures in the Hebrew (some Aramaic) and Greek languages. *Yet not one legitimate contradiction has been found among its pages.*

Dr. Robert Wilson of Princeton Seminary knew 14 ancient Middle Eastern languages like his own tongue. He testified that he had studied the Bible for over 40 years to find any contradiction. In that time he found none!

---

2. The Bible has predicted hundreds of prophecies, which have literally come true. All of the various countries, city states, as well as kings surrounding Israel were contained in these predictions, which came true. The life of Jesus was predicted hundreds of years before the events happened.

PROPHECY AND MATH

A mathematician told the odds of only thirteen predictions about Jesus being fulfilled. It would be like filling the state of Texas with silver dollars a mile high with one dollar marked in the mix. Then a blind person would be given one chance to find the marked dollar!
(Josh McDowell, *Evidence that Demands a Verdict*)

3, The Bible has been a source of joy, purpose and victory. It has transformed the most unlikely and the desperately defeated.

4. The Bible matches our intellectual needs and wins our hearts over, when we find out the love and sacrifice of Jesus, who died for our sins. (Dr. Peter Piper)

HOW DO WE INTERPRET THE BIBLE?

It might surprise many that the Bible was written so the average person could understand it! One of the hardest books of the Bible to understand is Revelation. Even that book promises that if a congregation will hear the Bible read and apply it, they will be blessed! (Revelation 1:3)

Here are three principles of interpretation:
1) Take a passage in its **PLAIN SENSE.**

What that means is you take it in its normal grammatical meaning. Read it in its context. Read about the background of the passage (we'll **get to this later on**.) Read up on certain words in the text with a commentary.

Some people make the bad mistake of declaring, *I won't read anything about the Bible, only the Bible itself!*

Sounds spiritual, doesn't it? However, it's really *prideful.* We are built up in our faith and understanding by other teachers. Some of them write commentaries and really know the Hebrew and Greek of the Scriptures. Some are faithful teachers and pastors. (Ephesians 4: 11-12). Some of them are godly men and women in a congregation that have walked with God for some time.

2) Take a passage in its **PROGRESSIVE SENSE**.

The Bible reveals its truth little by little. There are truths that are given in the early history of the Bible that are expanded on later on. This is particularly true of teaching and prophecy (Hebrews 1:1).

That's why we need to learn the background and pathway of Biblical history (which the Bible gives us).

The Old Testament has 17 books of history. Why? Because the God of the Bible stepped into history. He was involved and still is with our lives and His plan for us. So we need to know the setting and time when certain truths were uttered and how this applies to our age.

3) Take the Bible in its **PRACTICAL SENSE.**

When you read or study a section of Scripture, ask, "How does this apply to me?" As my son- in- law puts it, *so what?*

> **The president of our seminary told us, "You've had training in Hebrew, Greek, Bible, and Theology. When you go to your first church, sit under godly older men and women of your congregation, *who really know the Bible by experience!***

Many times you won't get that on your own. A group Bible study, a preacher, a book, or a word from a friend will really touch you through the Word of God. Sometimes we're not hard enough on ourselves. Other times we're too hard, and need the comforting principles and guidance from the Scripture.

WHAT HAS GOD BEEN DOING TO GET US TO WHERE WE ARE?

Let's start on the pathway where God began to lead the people of faith. So in the next chapter we're going to see this journey by the first book of the Bible. Plunge in! We're going to the very foundation of all we believe and our very purpose why we're on earth.

A Quick Guide through the Bible

Take a Look in Your Bible at the List of Books that
Make Up the Scriptures
Old Testament
17 Historical Books 5 Poetical Books 17 Prophetic
New Testament
5 Historical Books   21 Letters   1 Prophetic Book

Chapter Two:
GENESIS

Chapters 1:1-2:3, The Creation of the Heavens and Earth and Life

Chapters 2:4-5:35, The Garden of Eden and the Fall with Its Consequences

Chapters 6-9, The Flood

Chapters 10-11, The Tower of Babel

Chapters 12:1-25:18, The Life of Abraham & Isaac

Chapters 25:18-36:43, The Life of Jacob

Chapters 37-50, The Life of Joseph

We can honestly say, if people know little about Genesis, then their Bible knowledge is very limited!

The word *Genesis* means *beginning.* It comes from the first verse, **In the beginning God created the heavens and the earth** (Genesis 1:1). This just shows how the Scripture matches our need to know

.

Matter breaks down. It isn't eternal. Where did it come from? *God created.* Well who created God? No one! Nothing! God is an eternal being, and when he created he set cause and effect into play and time (sequence began).

The word for God is *Elohim,* which means
El =Power
Ho=Planner
Im=Plural
(Luepold's *Commentary on Genesis*)

The plural form speaks of His majesty and hints in later revelation of His triune nature. Yet, God is one, so the word *created* is singular.

Chapter 1 can be understood by the fact that creation is looked upon by gazing over the earth. *The Spirit of God moved upon the face of the deep* (Genesis 1:2).

In the beginning stages of creation the earth was *without form and void.* Using everyday English, the earth was Shapeless which the first three days address. The last three then fill the void or Emptiness left in the first three days.

SHAPELESS	EMPTY,
1. Light & Darkness	4. Moon, Sun, & Stars
Darkness	
2., Sky & Sea	5. Birds & Fish
3. Land and Trees	6. Animals & Humans

The seventh day God rested (where the word *Sabbath* comes from). The Lord ceased from creating, which gave an example to the Hebrews of resting after working six days. Also, they were once slaves in Egypt and couldn't rest.(**Exodus 20:11; 31:13; and Deuteronomy 5:15.**)

The Christian is not required to keep the Saturday Sabbath (Colossians 2:16). It was a special sign that Israel belonged to the Lord (Exodus 31:13).

Jesus once told his disciples to "come apart and rest awhile" (Mark 6:31). We need to leave the hectic pace of the world and on the Lord's day take time to worship, fellowship and rest. As Vance Havner once said, *If we don't come apart, we will come apart.*

TEMPTATION AND THE FALL

Chapter 2 in Genesis is a new section. It tells of the Garden of Eden which *God had planted* (Hebrew construction) for Adam and Eve. They were made in the image of God. That doesn't mean they looked like the Lord, because God is a spirit (John 4:24). It means that humans can rule the planet like God .Moreover, we have the capacity to understand God's revelation and moral standard.

The garden was made to train Adam, 1) to rule over the planet by working and naming the animals, 2) To understand marriage, and 3) to develop character by refraining eating from the

Tree of the Knowledge of Good and Evil. Even though created sinless, character must be developed. Our sinless Lord had to learn obedience and develop character (Genesis 2:15-28; Hebrews 5:8). The Garden was a Covenant (Hosea 2:18).

The Bible presents Adam and Eve as historic figures, even producing a genealogy. Our Lord spoke of them as historic real people. This is very important for the foundation for Christ making atonement for our sins.

> **Every human being possesses the same strands of mitochondrial DNA, coming from a single female and male. They even call them the *Adam and Eve DNA.***

Chapter 3 introduces the serpent, who is identified as Satan, the highest fallen Angel,(Revelation 12:9). The Devil incarnated a serpent-like creature, who was very beautiful. Eve yielded to the temptation of Satan, but Adam just went along with his wife, making his disobedience to God even worse.

SIN AND ITS CONSEQUENCES

Adam and Eve died spiritually that day. Isolated from God and His care, every offspring would be born without the spiritual work of God in their hearts. Sin, cruelty, pride and disharmony result in human life (**We are *dead in sins*,** Ephesians 2:5.).

The planet was also affected. Everything was out of balance by the curse: causing disease, famine, destruction,. (Romans 8:20-22).

The Tree of Life which contained nutrients, allowing eternal cellular reproduction, was kept from them. This resulted in physical death (Genesis 3:22-24).

GOOD NEWS IN THE GARDEN

The Lord announces that He will put **enmity,** meaning *hostility*, between the seed of the woman and the serpent. This word is used only regarding persons (Leupold). The term **seed of the woman** is highly unusual. It literally means *sperm of the woman*. This is a prophetic hint of the virgin birth of Jesus. The serpent's seed will strike the heel of the woman's seed, but the woman's seed will strike the head of the serpent (Genesis 3:15).

Another sign of grace is the covering of Adam and Eve with skins (Genesis 3:21). This demonstrated that substitutionary death was the only way guilt could be covered.

FROM THE FALL TO THE FLOOD
Genesis 7-10

Chapter 4 reports that Cain kills his brother. He travels to the land of Nod. His line produces many great achievements in building, industry, art, and power.

Why Does God Allow Bad Things?
1.The Fall. Adam, as the head of the human race, plunged us into disfavor and judgment and a sinful world (Genesis 3:8-11) 2. God knows what He's doing. I trust for the things I don't understand because He's proven Himself in the past (Job 40:1-5) 3. In judgment God is giving opportunity for repentance (Revelation 9:20-21) 4. God works good outcomes even from evil (Acts 4:27-28) 5. The Father wants everything to glorify the Son. His redemption glorifies His greatness and love (Philippians 2:5-11).

In Genesis 4:26, Seth another brother becomes a clan of godliness, worshipping God. In chapter 5:1-32, we have a genealogy of 10 generations. Even though the longevity is hundreds of years for each person, the familiar phrase after each one is *and he died.* One exception is Enoch, who walked with God and was taken to Him (v. 24). This illustrates that all of us will die as members of Adam's race. However, *Enoch is an illustration that some living believers will be caught up to meet the Lord when He comes.* They therefore like Enoch will never see physical death (I Corinthians 15:51).

Chapter 6 records that the Cain and Seth lines intermarry, producing a godless, violent, sinful human race

Constant iniquity and violence characterize human existence (vv. 5,13). In order to purge the iniquity and violence, God will judge the world by a flood. Only the family of Noah will be preserved.

The Flood

Chapters 7-9

Two objections to the flood narrative have been the *size of the waters* and *the size of the ark.*

There's enough water in the oceans to cover the earth a mile high. Moreover, the tectonic plates of the earth responding to earthquakes would bring about tsunamis creating waves hundreds of feet. However, on top of a tsunami the water is calm for the Ark to float.

Incidentally, some Christian geologists have speculated there may have been meteor bombardment on the earth during the flood. This would also cause great disturbances. We see that there was more than enough water.

Was the *size* of the ark big enough to hold all the animals? Engineers and international scientist have stated that the ark would be large enough to house all of today's land species. They would take up 28% of the Ark. Just as miraculously, the animals were called by God to go two by two on the ark, so they may have been in a state of semi-hibernation the year they lived on it.

THE COVENANT WITH NOAH

A *covenant* in Scripture is a legal act. The commands for the Garden of Eden are called a covenant (Hosea 6:7). It is similar to our term contract. The covenant with Noah is laid down by the Lord as a legislative act. It is still in force (Genesis 9:1-17).

It permits that animal protein may be consumed by humans, no doubt due to the lack of vegetation because of the flood.

It also stipulates that capital punishment must be given to anyone who murders a human being. The reason for this is that humans still bear the image of God even after the fall.

Lastly, God promises He will never destroy the earth with a world-wide flood. As a sign Noah sees the rainbow. Interestingly, the throne of God has a rainbow around it (Revelation 4:3). This shows that the Lord in giving judgment is never without mercy.

THE DISPERSEMENT OF THE NATIONS

At first the descendents of Noah would not follow the creation mandate and the

Covenant of Noah and go everywhere on the earth to live.

Chapter 11 tells how a rebellious race sought to build a city and a magnificent tower to show the glory of humankind (Genesis 11:1-8). The world's population probably numbered around 30,000 (Kiel and Delitch, *Commentaries of the Old Testament*).

God thwarted their efforts by changing the language miraculously into several; they could not understand each other so must disperse. The Lord does not want a uniform society with no variety. Such groups thwart the freedoms and creative/inventive abilities of those created in the image of God.

LANGUAGES

This does not mean that the Bible teaches all languages came by a miracle. In Genesis we read that various languages developed naturally in isolation to one another (Genesis 10:5).

However, there are families of languages that seem to possess totally different ways of uttering words. It appears they have no relationship to other language groups.

Yet, languages develop fairly rapidly naturally. Scientists have wondered why there are not more. The best explanation that there are fewer language groups than one would expect is to accept the history and time of Noah.

CHANGES IN THE HUMAN RACE

After the flood the ages recorded for humans are *drastically reduced.* By the time we come to Moses, he writes the average age was 70 to 80 years, fairly close to our day, 3500 years from Moses (Psalm 90:10).

I believe there's a simple explanation for this. Adam and Eve were the beginners who had a large store of variety of genes for the human race. When we come to Noah, we have a segment of the origin of the human race. The weaknesses and defects of Noah's family were passed on. It's like taking a duplicate paper and reproducing it. The duplicate cannot produce as many quality images as the original.

Another change has to do with the various *races.* The idea of great differences in races is scientifically laughable. There's only one race. All humans have very little differences. In fact we can give blood (A, B, AB, O types) to any one of any race. The differences are simply familial traits and adaptive traits from the environment. Skin color usually means an ancestry that was either closer to or farther away from the equator.

When God created the various kinds of animals, they were given capacities for variation. A feline can breed into a variety of cats, but they're still cats.   Dogs have a fantastic variety, but they are all dogs and can interbreed. Horses can be ponies, huge Clydesdales, or zebras, but all can mate with one another. So with humans, they can have slight variations of skin color, eye shape, height, hair but *all belong to the human race.* We are one race made in the image of God, but also sinners, who need a Savior.

GOD BEGINS A NEW PROGRAM

Chapters 12-22

The Lord is never called the "God of Adam, Seth, and Noah."   He's **the God of Abraham, Isaac, and Jacob** (Exodus 3:6).

The Lord in Abraham began His kingdom on earth. Now we come to a major covenant in Scripture. (The major covenants are the key to understanding the Bible.) Here's one   that changes all of history and our present day. We have read about the Edenic Covenant, the Noahic Covenant, now we will examine the *Abrahamic Covenant* (Genesis 12-17).

THE CALL OF THE COVENANT

The Lord calls Abraham out of the Pagan lands and practices to follow Him (Chapter 12:1-3). Hebrews 11:8 lists this step as an example of faith.

Genesis 12:2-3 gives promises to Abraham that the Lord would make out of him a **great nation.** The first time the word *nation* is used in the Bible. Out of this *all the families of the earth will be blessed.*

The 7 Promises Given to Abraham in vv. 2-3

1. God will make of Abraham a great nation

2. God will bless Abraham

3. God will make Abraham's name great

4. Abraham will be a great blessing

5. God will bless those who bless Abraham

6. God will curse those who curse Abraham

7. In Abraham will all earth's families blessed

THE CONNECTION TO THE COVENANT

The Lord tells Abraham that his biological seed will be numerous like the stars in the sky. Abraham believed that promise and revelation from God. *He believed in the Lord, and He counted it to him for righteousness* (15:3).

This is the way God saves anybody in all ages. They must trust in the promise He has revealed to them. In this case Abraham believed in what was to become of his offspring. In the progress of revelation from the Bible, we see this is ultimately fulfilled in Jesus Christ (Galatians 3:16)

Abraham illustrates what true faith is. He forsook his own way of living and turned in trust to the Lord. He also believed the promise of God, which would culminate in Christ's death for our sins. Did he understand what we know today in the light of the New Testament? No. I am sure He knew nothing of a Messiah, His death, and resurrection. That was revelation to come. However, while the *content* of his faith was less than ours, the *object* was the same.

What Is the Content of our Faith Today?

Christ died for our sins, according to the Scripture (I Corinthians 15:3)

He was buried and rose again the third day, according to the Scriptures (I Corinthians 15:4)

Repent and believe the gospel (Mark 1:15).

(A willingness to turn from sin, and trust in Jesus for forgiveness and eternal life.)

THE CONFIRMATION OF THE COVENANT
Genesis 15:7-21

Abraham takes two halves of animals and separates them so two parties can walk between the animals and establish a covenant. However, Abraham stands outside and only God appears by the sign of smoke and fire. This shows that *only God makes the covenant.*

The Lord tells Abraham that his offspring will serve in a nation (Egypt). After 400 years his offspring will leave that land and be the instruments of judgment to Canaan. God is willing to wait, giving the Amorites (the most prominent tribe, standing for all of Canaan) to repent.

The Lord then promises to give the land of Canaan to the offspring of Abraham.

THE CIRCUMSSISION SIGN OF THE COVENANT
Genesis 17;1-14

Abraham is reassured that the Covenant God made with Him is *eternal* (v.7). He then is commanded to make sure that every male, 8 days old and older, be circumcised. This shows a personal testimony for every male that he is a part of the supernatural covenant.

THE LIFE OF ABRAHAM

Abraham, the father of the faith, does falter at times. This is an encouragement to us that the Lord is merciful when we fall, and works with us to become stronger in Him. One horrible move is when Sarah convinces Abraham that his offspring will come from her maid (a pagan practice of the time). The offspring is Ishmael, who forms part of the Arab family. The two offspring are enemies to this day (Genesis 16)

Abraham rescues his nephew Lot by fighting against those who kidnapped him. He then meets a mysterious king and priest of the Lord. The priest, **Melchizedek,** is given a tenth of Abraham's bounty. *This shows that the pattern of giving a tenth to the Lord was established over 400 years before the Law was enacted* (Genesis 14:18-20). The Bible teaches that Christ's Priesthood is like Melchizedek, directly appointed , not conferred by inheritance.. Christ was not a Priest after the Mosaic Law, which required being part of the tribe of Levi. (Psalm 110:4; Hebrews 7:3).

Sodom, where Lot lives, is a city of iniquity, including guilt of homosexuality and rape. God judges this city by bringing down fire and sulfur upon it. Lot's wife becomes a *pillar of salt* when by earthquake and explosions of gas and oil, salt, fire and sulfur, came raining down. She had stayed too close and looked fondly at the world she was leaving. These pillars can still be observed in the area. Jesus uses this passage to warn those with only a nominal faith. She longed for the wicked life-style of Sodom (Luke 17:32).

. Sarah finally, miraculously, bears a son to Abraham as an older Woman (Genesis 21:2).

Abraham becomes strong in faith and is willing to sacrifice his son, Isaac to the Lord. He believed that God could raise him from the dead (Genesis 22:1-14; Hebrews 11:17).

ABRAHAM'S OFFSPRING

Isaac, who is born to Abraham and Sarah, (Genesis 21),marries Rebekah (Chapter 24). (Read the wonderful story how the Lord led Abraham's servant to find her). Isaac and Rebekah have twins Esau and Jacob. Esau has little use for his parent's faith and his birthright as the eldest. Favoritism exists as Isaac prefers Esau. Rebekah is more attached to Jacob.

Rebekah overhears blind Isaac is going to give Esau the family blessing as the firstborn, which include spiritual and material inheritance. Isaac requests that Esau go out and hunt game and prepare him a delicious meal. Rebekah hurriedly makes a meal for her husband and has Jacob disguise himself as Esau. The deception works, and Isaac gives Jacob the firstborn blessing (Genesis 27).

In bitter anger Esau is overheard by Rebekah that he intends to murder his brother. She dispatches Jacob to go live with her brother Leban. He turns out to be as deceptive as Jacob

.

Jacob agrees to work for Leban for seven years, so he may marry his younger daughter Rachel. Leban tricks Jacob and he marries the veiled older sister Leah. Jacob then must work another seven years to have Rachel, which he marries right away. Though treating Leah harshly, she nevertheless bears him many children. In a superstitious act Rachel receives a mandrake root from Leah. She conceives and bears Joseph. All in all, between the two wives and their two maids, twelve sons are born. These will eventually grow in 400 years to become the twelve tribes of Israel.

Leban takes sheep and goats from Jacob, and tells him he can only keep speckled or spotted goats and speckles, spotted, or black sheep. He then removes such type of sheep and goats from his flocks. Jacob, then, makes speckled tree limbs and puts them near watering troughs. He naively thinks this will make the offspring of his herds speckled colored. Indeed, such kinds of lambs and kids multiply. However, the *Lord tells him that it was He, God, who increased his flocks* (Genesis 31:11-13). He reminds Jacob of his half-hearted faith, when he had replied to the Lord that he would serve Him if He prospered him.

The Lord is not finished with Jacob. As he is returning home with his wives, sons, and livestock, he hears that his brother Esau is coming to him with 400 men. He separates his family, and then waits alone for his brother. That night he wrestles with the Angel of the Lord, seemingly *controlling* him. However, his thigh is touched and sprained. Jacob then can only *hold* on. He is then changed from trying to control God's plan to just holding on to the Lord. He is given the name *Israel,* meaning struggler with God (Genesis 32:28).

Esau meets Jacob, but does not seek revenge, but lovingly embraces him as a brother. Did God change Esau's heart overnight when Jacob wrestled with the Angel of the Lord? Or had Esau long forgotten his bitterness? We don't know, *but we do know God changed Jacob that night.*

THE 12 SONS OF JACOB
Genesis 33-50

Ten of the sons of Jacob are rogues. His first son born to Racael, Joseph, is a Godly young man and his favorite. His brothers hate him, and after beating him up, they sell him at the age of 17 to the Arabs as a slave. Brought to Egypt, he then is falsely accused of attempted rape and thrown into prison. As a prophet, he predicts 7 years of prosperity and 7 years of severe famine. Pharaoh of Egypt then makes Joseph, who is now 3O years old, in charge of collecting the grain for storage, and then for distribution in the coming famine

During the famine, his older brothers go to Egypt to purchase grain for their starving household. They do not recognize their brother. Joseph wisely keeps from revealing himself and brings about conditions that force them to acknowledge their sins. His "tough love" pays off, because the brothers show signs of repentance.

Joseph reveals himself and makes arrangements for his father, Jacob, and the 11 brothers to live in Egypt with their families. The total number is seventy people. Preserved from starvation they grow from twelve clans, to tribes and finally a nation of people while in Egypt.

Joseph acknowledges to all that with his trials, his brothers meant it for evil, but God meant it for good (**Genesis 37-50**). *God's intentions are always greater than evil's.*

In my book *A Clear Guide to Genesis*, I report that students of the Word found 18 similarities of Joseph's life and Christ's.

See how many can be found in your reading?

Chapter Three:
FROM CAPTIVITY TO THE
WILDERNESS
Exodus-Deuteronomy

EXODUS:
   Chapters 1-6, Moses' Background and Calling.

   Chapters 7-18, The Plagues and the Departure from Egypt

   Chapters 19-40, Coming to Mount Sinai and Receiving the Law

   Exodus tells us there arose a king who didn't know Joseph. The Israelites are made slaves in Egypt. However, they continue to multiply, worrying the Egyptian royalty, that they might create an uprising. One pharaoh orders that all male Israelite babies be killed on delivery. However, the Egyptian midwives are godly, and do not obey the king, but the Lord (1:1-22).

   Moses' parents hid their baby in a box, hidden by the reeds in the river. A princess of the pharaoh was bathing nearby and found the baby.

   At once her maternal heart was touched and decided to adopt the baby. She called the baby *Moses,* which in Egyptian means *child,* but in Hebrew, *to be drawn out.* The princess calls to

Moses' sister to find a nurse for the child. (I am sure she knew full well that the child would bring Moses' mother) (2:1-10)

Moses grows up in the palace of the Pharoah. At 40 years he sees a Hebrew being beaten by an Egyptian. Moses strikes the Egyptian, killing him. He finds out that his act has been told to many. Fearing for his life he flees Egypt for Midian, where he becomes a shepherd for Jethro, a priest, and marries his daughter and lives as a family-man for 40 years (2:11-22).

One day God calls Moses out of a burning bush that is not consumed. The Lord tells Moses, he has been called to lead Israel out of Egypt. He tells them to use the sacred name for God, *I am That I am.* This name is translated in our English Bibles with the full capitals *LORD.* The Hebrew seems to convey that *the Lord is the only God and all existence comes from Him.* Some Hebrew scholars think it also has the meaning, *God will faithfully carry out all He declares* (3:1-22).

The Lord gives Moses signs to show that He is the chosen leader to deliver them from Egyptian slavery. If he puts his hand into his clothing his hand turns white as leprosy. It becomes normal when he puts it back into his clothing. He is given a rod that becomes a snake when he casts it down. When he picks it up, it becomes a rod again. These sign miracles are prevalent when the Lord starts a new program.

Moses is also given Aaron, his brother, to help him speak before Pharaoh (4:1-18).

Chapters 7-18); The 10 Plagues and the Departure from Egypt.

Pharaoh will not permit the Israelites to leave Egypt to worship God. Therefore, Moses warns of several plagues. Pharaoh at times seems like he will give in. Then he has second thoughts, no doubt believing that these plagues are only coincidences and not from the Hebrew God (Exodus 7-12).

The 10 Plagues
1 .Nile River turns
to blood.
2. Frogs invade
land
3. Lice invade land
4. Flies invade
land
5. Disease of
cattle
6. Disease of boils
7. Great hail
8. Multitude of
locusts
9. Great Darkness
10. Death of the
First-born

Archeologist Cameron has found similar plagues in the world. However, the miracles were in the *timing* and the *specific applications*. None of the Israelites were affected, but their Egyptian neighbors were.

During the night the Israelites observed the Passover feast. On their front door blood was dabbed from the sacrificial lamb. It was smeared on the top, sides, and entrance way (making a cross). The New Testament tells us that Christ is our Passover, who died that we will live.

CROSSING THE RED SEA

In Exodus 14, the Lord leads the Israelites to the shores of the Red Sea. Pharaoh has sent his army with chariots to subdue them and bring them back to Egypt. God tells Moses to stretch his hands over the sea. The Lord sends a strong wind that causes a dry pathway through the sea. The Israelites pass over, but the Egyptians pursue with chariots. However, God tells Moses to stretch out his hand. The waters begin to close together and the army of Egypt is drowned.

> ### Archeologists May Have Found the Site of the Crossing of the Red Sea
> A sand bridge connecting the west and east banks of the Red Sea has been found, several feet below sea level. The wind could very well blow the water from one side of the bridge over to the other (making two pools or pillars). The shallow water removed would make a bridge to the other side.
> Also found were remnants of chariots.

MOUNT SINAI AND THE GIVING OF THE LAW
Chapter 19-40

The Lord takes Moses up into the Mountain to reveal His law. The purpose of the Law was to show them the Lord's *standard* to guide their lives, to make them a *unique culture* in how they dressed and ate, to guide them as a nation in their *civil* laws, and to instruct them in their *worship*, especially their *need for pardon* through the many sacrifices. *The spiritual intent of the law was to show them they were sinners and in need of the grace of God.* This grace symbolized in their rituals was fully realized in the life and death of Jesus (Hebrews 10;3-4, 10)

THE TEN COMMANDMENTS
Exodus 20:3-17; Deuteronomy 5:7-21

1. No other gods, but God
2. No idols
3. Do not take God's Name in vain
4. Remember the Sabbath
5. Honor your parents
6. Do not murder
7. Do not commit adultery
8. Do not steal
9. Do not bear false witness
10. Do not covet

THE MAKING OF THE TABERNACLE,
Exodus 25-40

After giving basic civil laws, Moses then explains the Tabernacle, the place all Israel shall worship. The Tabernacle was symbolic of heavenly worship and of Jesus as our High Priest (Hebrews 8:1-7 ; 9:1-14). It was a giant rectangle which could be set up at each stop where the Israelites traveled. The outer court had place for cleansing and an altar for sacrifice.

The inner section was the Holy Place. This was divided into two sections. The first area only priests could enter and had the 12 lamps for each tribe, and table for bread the priests would eat, and an altar of incense showing continual adoration and communion with the Lord.

The most holy place (Holy of Holies) the second section of the Holy Place, could only be entered by the high priest as he came with the blood of atonement for sins, The room contained the ark of the covenant. On its lid blood was sprinkled. This blood came from a slain bull. When Jesus was crucified, an earthquake tore the curtain separating the holy of holies from the outer court. This pictured that Jesus now opened by His death the way for all of us to possess direct access to God.(Matthew 27:51; Hebrews 9:8, 24).

LEVITCUS tells us of

Laws of Offerings, **Chapters 1-7**

Laws of the Priests, **Chapters 8-10**

Laws of Purification, **Chapters 11-15**

Law for Day of Atonement, **Chapter 16**

Laws for Separation, **Chapters 17-22**

Laws of Feasts, Booths, Tabernacle and Land, **Chapters 23-25**

Blessing, Curses, Vows, **Chapters 26-27**

THE MAIN OFFERINGS

The Burnt Offering for sin, pictures Christ's Once for All death for us

The Meal Offering illustrates thanksgiving for all God's provisions

The Peace Offering illustrates that we have peace with God through Christ's sacrifice

The Sin and Trespass Offerings illustrate that Christ's death epardons us from unintentional sins, due to the hardness of our hearts.

THE CELEBRATIONS BY FEASTS

Passover celebrated Israel's deliverance from slavery and illustrates our deliverance through Christ from the slavery of sin (I Corinthians 5:7).

Unleaven Bread, it illustrates that Christ, the Bread of Life, is without the contamination of sin (I Corinthians 15:21)

First Fruits expressed that all of the harvest of barley is from God, and illustrates that Christ was the first yield in His resurrection, and we are to follow (I Corinthians 15:20-23).

Pentecost was the seventh Sabbath after the First Fruits Feast to commemorate the first yield of wheat. It reminds us that the Holy Spirit came and baptized the church on that feast (its spiritual birthday) and many were brought into Christ's kingdom (Acts 2:1-47).

Trumpets (Rosh Hashanna) was the first day of the seventh month, sanctifying the seventh month or Sabbath Month. Some see this illustrating the trumpet sound when Christ comes for His people (ICorinthians15:52, Beechek , *Pretribulational Rapture,*)

Day of Atonement (Yom Kippur) made animal sacrifice for the Sins of the people and priests, illustrating Christ's once-for-all sacrifice for our sins (Hebrews 9:1-28)

Feast of Booths was observed from the 15th to the 22nd days of the seventh month commemorating the time Israel spent in the wilderness under God's protection and celebrating the gathering of the harvest. Illustrates our being gathered to Jesus when He comes again (I Thessalonians 4:16-17)

(Bill Jones, *Putting Together the Puzzle of the Old Testament*, Horatio Bonar, *Christ in the Old Testament*).

NUMBERS tells us of the wilderness wandering of the Israelites.

Chapters 1-3, The Census

Chapters 4-10, Duties of Levites and Legal and Ritual duties

Chapters 11-12, Departure from Sinai to Paran near Canaan

Chapters 13-14, the Sending of the 12 spies into Canaan and the people's rebellion to invade,

Chapters 15-25, After the People rebelled about conquering the land of Canaan., that generation over 20 year of age wandered the wilderness for 40 years until they all died out, except Joshua and Caleb. They had urged the people to trust the Lord and conquer Canaan,

During this time God fed the people with the miraculous food called *manna,* (means, *what is it?*)

.

Chapters 26-36, Preparation is made 40 years afterward for entering Canaan with the generation born after the rebellion. Joshua and Caleb remained alive, and Joshua becomes the successor of Moses.

DEUTERONOMY means *Second Law.*

The book is a rehearsal of the laws for the new generation, which were previously given at Sinai.

The format is very much like a written covenant, which was the style of such documents in 1406 B.C.

Person's Involved in the Covenant 1:1-5
A Review of Past Relations 1:6-4:49
Basic Stipulations of the treaty, 5:1-26:19
Sanctions of Blessing and Curses, 27:1-30:20
Witnesses, 32:1
Provision of Storage and Reading 31:1-34:12

(The Nelson Study Bible)

Deuteromy is not slavishly written just like a covenant, as it adds further details and teachings for God's people.

Chapters 1:1-4:43 is a review of the 40 year history of Israel in the wilderness

Chapters 4:44-11:32 is a review of the Law
The Ten Commandments are repeated (5:6-22).

Chapters 12-26 gives the organization of civil life

Chapters 27-30 A call to keep the Covenant

Chapters 31-33, Joshua replaces Moses

IS THERE A CONTRADICTION IN THE 10 COMMANDMENTS?

Exodus 20:11 states that the Israelites were to keep the Sabbath because God rested on the Seventh Day of Creation.

Deuteronomy 5:15 states that the Israelites should remember they were slaves in Egypt and had no day of rest

The answer is easy. The command on stone was to remember the Sabbath Day. *Moses inspired Comments were his application for keeping the Sabbath. These were not on the stone tablets but in his writings of Exodus and Deuteronomy.*

Chapter Four:
CONQUERING AND LIVING IN CANAAN:
Joshua-Ruth

JOSHUA

Chapters 1-12, Records the conquest of Canaan, which includes the parting of the Jordan River, which swells a mile wide in the spring. Also, there is spiritual preparation, and the realization they are on God's side.

Two spies are sent out into the land. Rahab, a female innkeeper of Jericho (usually implying a prostitute, as well) believes the Lord will give the city to Israel. She obtains the promise from the spies that her life and that of her family will be spared. Rahab marries an Israelite and is listed in Jesus' genealogy (Matthew 1:5).

Also, the great miraculous victory over Jericho takes place when the Israelites march around the city and the walls cave (Chapter 6).

Another spectacular miracle was the lengthening of the Day (Chapter 10) There are all kinds of speculation how God did this, but it was a day never occurred before or since.

Chapters 13-22: the Divisions of the Land to the 12 Tribes.

However, not all the Canaanites are driven out of the land, which becomes a burden and temptation to compromise their faith in coming generations.

Chapters 23-24, The Farewell Address of Joshua and death..

The book of Joshua takes place over 25 years. For a whole generation after Joshua's death the Israelites served God

.

JUDGES tells us of the horrible pattern of life that occurred under the Judges. After the generation that followed Joshua, there arose another that did not know Joshua or the Lord.

One great problem was that a godly generation would not pass on the truth of God or lessons learned to the next. It's been well-said that Christianity is always one generation away from extinction.

> Take some time to read Deuteronomy six. Reflect on the best way we as parents and grandparents can teach the children the faith.

The pattern throughout Judges 340 years is REBELLION, RUIN, REPENTANCE, RESTORATION.

The people would follow the gods and culture of the pagans living among them in *rebellion* against the Law of God. This would lead to the pagans taking control and bringing hardship and poverty. The people would cry out to the Lord in their *ruin*.

Chapters 1-16 God raised up *Judges* who would lead the Israelites to *repent* and follow the Lord, breaking off the yolk of their oppressors. This brought about *restoration*.

Of the 13 Judges recorded 10 had to lead the Israelites into battle. There are three judges that stand out.

Deborah was a prophetess and judge. She led her people against Jabin, the king of the Canaanites, and battled Sisera, their captain through her military assistant, Barak. She ruled for 40 years (Chapters 4-5). This shows that woman can be perfectly equipped to lead in governmental and political roles, as well as business (Proverbs 31:16-20; Acts 16:14-15).

Gideon was a farmer, who was led to overthrow the oppression of the Midianites, Amalekites, and the Children of the East (Judges 6-8). God made him to reduce his army of 32,000 to only 300 men.

At night Gideon instructed his 300 men to surround the camp and cover their torches. At an arranged signal they were to show their torches, blow their horns, and shout, *the sword of the Lord and Gideon!* (Judges 7:10-25). The Midianites panicked and in the dark began fighting and killing their colleagues. Gideon ruled his people for 40 years. This showed that the Lord can use the most unlikely people who step by step trust him.

Samson was dedicated to God by His parents, who raised him as a Nazarite (Chapter 13). This was a vow to the Lord by a male to live a life separated to God. Usually the vow was for a short time. The Nazarite was not to eat grapes, drink any substance that was fermented, not to touch any corpse, animal or human, and not cut his hair. He also spent major time communing with God, meditating and following His law, and worship (Numbers 6:1-21)
.

Samson did not live a separate or moral life at all. The only area he obeyed was not cutting his hair, which was supposed to show he was dedicated over to the Lord. The Holy Spirit honored that appearance and gave him supernatural strength to carry on the judgment of God against the Philistines. However, his acts of judgments were of little consideration for Israel or the Lord, but his own personal vengeance (Chapters 13-16).

THE FAMOUS HAIRCUT

Samson has his famous encounter with a prostitute Delilah in the valley of Sorek (Chapter 16:4-31). She asks him to reveal the secrets of his strength, and he finally tells it is due to his hair. (However, it was due to his outward profession to all that he belongs to the Lord. His power is only from Him.)

Delilah cuts his hair while Samson sleeps, and sadly, *He did not know that the Lord was departed from him* (vv.16:20). He is beaten, blinded and enchained with brass. He ends up like an animal, moving the grinding stone in the Philistine prison.

When the Philistines gathered in that area to worship their god Dagon, Samson was brought out and stood near the supporting pillars of their temple. There, he and the Lord were mocked, and the Dagon extolled. But Samson praying to the Lord took hold of the supporting pillars and the whole temple came crashing down, killing Samson and those in attendance. More Philistines were killed than the total of Samson's past exploits.

Samson had ruled 20 years, Chapters 13-16. His work did not deliver the Israelites from the Philistines, but began that effort.

Chapters 17-21 records almost in despair ending with one deed after the other of depravity, idolatry, and rash judgments (Chapters 17-21). The book ends with a phrase repeated 17:6; 18:1; 19:1, and 21:25, *In those days there was no king in Israel: every man did what was right in his own eyes.*

Archeological digs have unearthed Philistine temples. Usually people congregated inside and on the roof of the Temple, supported by key pillars. This illustrates the destruction visited by Samson pushing down those supports.

RUTH is a short book that brings some relief to the horrible 340 years of Judges.

Chapters 1-2, we see godliness exhibited in the most unlikely person. Due to a famine an Israelite family with two sons take up residence in Moab. The two sons marry Moabite women. The father and sons die, leaving Naomi the mother and her two daughters in law alone. Naomi **goes** back to Israel, accompanied by the Moabite Ruth, widow of Naomi's son. Ruth refuses to leave her or the Lord.

Chapters 3-4, destitute, Ruth gleans barley in the fields. The Lord provides the field of a distant relative of Naomi, the field of Boaz. Ruth and Boaz fall in love. However, Boaz cannot marry her until a closer relative agrees not to act as a kinsman redeemer and marry her. Happily, he agrees and Boaz marries Ruth. He takes care of her mother-in-law as well. Ruth is also recorded in the royal line of David and the Lord (Ruth 4:17; Matthew 1:5).

I & II SAMUEL, I & II KINGS, I & II CHRONICLES

In the next section we will see how the Lord set up kings to carry out his will. We'll also see the failures and even the destruction of Israel and the captivities.

However, this is all a preparation for the one who comes. The King of Kings, Jesus Christ the Lord

---

Chapter Five:
THE TIME OF THE KINGS
I Samuel-II Chronicles

I SAMUEL tells us of Life of Samuel, Saul, and David in his younger years.

Chapters 1-8, Samuel was a prophet, priest, and ruler (judge). In a real sense he was a picture of Christ, who is our Prophet, Priest, and King
.

Samuel's sons were corrupt, so the Israelite demanded he give them a king like the other nations.

The Lord tells Samuel that they are rejecting not Samuel but God to rule over them (v.7).
Now the Lord already had prophesied that Israel would have a king. However, the standard was for one who would be guided by the Word of God over him (Deuteronomy 17:18-2

Chapters 9-15, Saul is chosen to be king, and he starts off fairly well. However, he begins to disobey the Lord and even takes it upon himself to act as a Priest. Saul is told that God has rejected him and his dynasty as king (Chapter 13:13-14).

Chapter 16-31, David, a shepherd lad is prophetically anointed to be king by Samuel (16:13). He eventually is hired to play for King Saul. His music soothes the erratic temper of the king.

David's most famous feat is the *killing of the giant Goliath by a stone in his sling* (Chapter 17). As David grows he becomes a great warrior, and Saul seeks to kill him, believing David will usurp him. David spends many years outside of Israel, often escaping Saul. King Saul and his son are eventually killed in battle (Chapters 18-31).

THEOCRACY	MONARCHY
GOD & HIS WORD RULES, TAUGHT BY PRIESTS.	THE KING RULES AND IS NOT SUBJECT TO ANYONE OR GOD.
KING RULES UNDER GOD AND SUBJECT TO GOD'S WORD.	HE ALSO MAY BECOME A PRIEST.
THE PEOPLE ARE GOVERNED BY THE KING ONLY AS FAR AS THE WORD PERMITS.	THE PEOPLE ARE GOVERNED BY THE KING AND HIS ARBITRARY COMMANDS.

II SAMUEL tells us of David rule

,**Chapters 1-11**. He first rules in Judah (Chapters 1-3) and then all Israel (Chapters 4-24). Under his rule many of Israel's enemies are defeated. He captures Jerusalem and makes it the capital of Israel. He also rescues the ark of the covenant from the Philistines. In Chapter 7:16-17 God makes a covenant with David that his offspring will rule Israel forever. This is fulfilled in Jesus Christ. (See also Psalm 89).

However, King David commits adultery with Bathsheba, the wife of Uriah the Hittite, who serves in David's army. Bathsheba becomes pregnant. David tries to bring Uriah home to his wife. Uriah a loyal soldier will not leave the battle, so David arranges for him to serve in a dangerous section where he is killed (Chapter 11)..

Chapters 12-20 David's sin is discovered by Nathan the prophet. David earnestly seeks God through repentance (Chapter 12).. His seeking restoration and forgiveness can be read in Psalm 51.

> **This is a great Psalm to read often, not only for major situations of sin, but daily confession of our sins, as we're commanded in I John 1:9-10**

Though forgiven, David's child by Bathsheba dies. Moreover, he faces many enemies attacking Israel. He also faces a revolt by his son Absalom, who forces him to flee his throne in Jerusalem. However, Absalom is killed and David returns to his throne(Chapters 14-19). Later, he faces another revolt under Sheba (Chapter 20).

I KINGS

Chapters 1-11 tell us of the last days of David and the kingship of Solomon, born of Bathsheba. Solomon's beginning kingship is rocky. He faces a competitor, Adonijah, another son of David.

However, Solomon is made king, and God favors him with special wisdom and expands and provides for his kingdom more than at any time in Israel's history. Israel becomes wealthiest of all the lands in the Middle East. The expansion and trade of Israel was the greatest in their history before or since (Chapters 5-10).

Solomon builds the Temple for the Lord,(Chapters 5-10). He acknowledges that *the heaven and heavens cannot contain Thee, how much less this house that I have built* (Chapter 8:27). This magnificent structure should have been called one of the wonders of the world. On the day of dedication the presence of the Lord is seen in a cloud, so thick that the priests could not minister (Chapter 8:10-11)

Solomon's prayer (Chapter 8:22-53) and his remarks to Israel afterward (vv. 54-61) should be reviewed. In it he asks that the heathen (Gentiles) who pray near the Temple will have their prayers answered so that they know the Lord is the true God (vv. 42-43). So the Temple has been given to draw not only Israelites but the Gentiles to know the Lord.

OLD TESTAMENT WORLD WIDE MISSION

The seed of the woman will strike the head of the Serpent, Genesis 3:15

The population from Noah should spread to the world with God's truth, Genesis 9:7

Abraham's seed to be a world-wide blessing, Genesis 12:3

The Temple at Jerusalem was to be a focal point for the Nations to learn of God

The dispersion of th Jews after the captivity spread the knowledge of God and was the forerunner of Christian Churches.

In direct disobedience from God's Word (Deuteronomy 17:14-20), Solomon multiplies horses (war animals), wives, silver and gold. Also, we wonder if these areas would not have been transgressed, if Solomon had repeated reminders of God's Word by reading it daily (vv. 18-19).

We Need to Take Time Each Day in the Word.

Have a special time to read a portion of the Word and ask, "What has that to do with me?"

A good discipline for us all, is "No Bible, no breakfast." "Take two verses before going to bed, and call on the Lord in the morning."

Solomon gains 700 wives and 300 concubines (mistresses) through treaties with various kings (Chapter 11:1-8). Eventually, to please his wives and concubines, he erects pagan shrines for them and even participated by accompanying them to their worship. So the king who was given a special gift of wisdom, and actually wrote 3000 proverbs and 1005 songs (Chapter 4:29-34) horribly ended his rule with compromise and sin.

Solomon finally came to his sense., In his old age he wrote the book of Ecclesiastes, where he concluded that all is vanity except to fear and obey God was *whole duty of man* (Ecclesiastes 12:13).The United Kingdom under the kings ends with Solomon. A good way to remember this period is

SAUL HAD NO HEART FOR GOD.
DAVID WAS WHOLE HEARTED FOR GOD
SOLOMON WAS HALF HEARTED FOR GOD.
(Bill Jones, *Putting Together the Puzzle of the Old Testament)*

. THE DIVIDED KINGDOM

Chapters 12-22, the son of Solomon, was confronted with the Israelites to ease up on the excessive taxes and excessive demands for service .Solomon had required Rehoboam consulted his elders, who advised him to ease up. However, his younger companions advised him to become tougher on the people and show his authority. Consequently, the 10 tribes of the north revolted and took Jeroboam as king. Only Judah and Benjamin remained (I Kings 12:1-25).

Jeroboam became king of the northern 10 tribes. He believed that the pilgrimages to Jerusalem to worship at the Temple would draw the tribes back into one nation. So he erected a temple and instituted golden calf worship.

The Northern Kingdom continued in idolatry though God sent the prophets Elijah and Elisha to call them to repentance. This was accompanied by many sign miracles. The ministry of Elijah is recorded in I Kings 17-22.

II KINGS records the history of the two kingdoms'

Chapters 1-2 records the dynasty of Jeroboam.

Chapters 3-8, highlights the ministry of Elisha the successor of Elijah.

Chapters 9-24 describes the dynasties of the two kingdoms with the Assyrian and Babylonian captivities.

NORTHERN KINGDOM
19 KINGS, ALL EVIL
SOUTHERN KINGDOM,
20 KINGS, SEVEN GOOD
The Northern Kingdom had several dynasties, often one killing off the other. The Southern Kingdom continued the Davidic line.

One great exception among the kings of Judah was Josiah (II Kings 22:-23). Josiah ruled when the *Book of the Law (Exodus-Deuteronomy)* was found hidden in the Temple. Josiah was greatly alarmed by the curses that were foretold by disobedience to God's law.

He took out all the idols from the temple and on its grounds. He also destroyed idol shrines in the countryside and reinstituted the Passover feast. He chased out the spiritualists and pagan ritualists from the land. **II Kings 23:25** tells us that there was no king before or since Josiah who turned to the Lord *with all his heart, with all his soul, and with all his might* (23:25).

Nevertheless, Josiah's reforms did not stay the judgment of God, as the people went right back to their sinful ways after his death.

> Many times people will labor for the Lord and few actually follow him. Success is in the Lord's hands. All we need to hear from the Savior is *"WELL DONE THOU GOOD AND FAITHFUL SERVANT"* (MATTHEW 25:21).

CAPTIVITY

The Lord in judgment allowed the Northern Kingdom to be conquered by Assyria and the ten tribes were led into captivity in 722 B.C. (II Kings 17:5-41).

The Lord in judgment allowed the Southern Kingdom to fall from 605 B.C. to 586 B.C, by Babylon. There were three assaults and three captivities. At the last campaign the Temple and Jerusalem were destroyed (II Kings 24-25).

I and II CHRONICLES were written for the exiles of the Babylonian captivity. It mostly excludes the history of the Northern Kingdom.

WHY DID GOD ALLOW THE CAPTIVITIES?

God must punish sin. However, out of the captivities Israel no longer ever resorted to blatant idolatry as it had in the past.

God was also preparing for a new dispensation, the church age. The example of Daniel and Esther would show how the Lord's people must serve among the Gentiles.

Those who returned to Israel gave a place for the Messiah to be born. The Jews scattered throughout the Roman world would become launching pads for the church.

I CHRONICLES, Chapters 1-9, The geneology of the tribes, Jerusalem, and Saul's ancestors.

Chapters 10-16, history of David's kingship.

Chapters 17-29, David's instructions and preparation for building the Temple.

II CHRONICLES, Chapters 1-9 Tells of the accomplishments of Solomon's rule.

Chapters 10-36, gives a history of Judah's kings, beginning with Rehoboam to the captivity. It also mentions that Manassah, the most wicked of all Israel's kings, repented at the end of his life (II Chronicles33).

Chapter Six:
REBUILDING AND EXILE
Ezra, Nehemiah, & Esther

EZRA tells us what happened after the captivity of Babylon lasting seventy years. **Chapters 1-6,** The Babylonian were defeated by the Medo-Persian Empire. The Emperor Cyrus in 538 B.C. allowed those in captivity to return to their lands and build temples and altars to their gods. Israel was also given such a decree. 50,000 returned to Jerusalem and the building of the Temple was begun in 536 B.C. (Chapters 1-3).

> Jeremiah 25:11-12, predicts the captivity will last seventy years.
>   The first phase took place in 605 B.C. and the building of the Temple was in 536 B.C. Precisely 70 years. (Extra year comes with transition from 6th century to the 5th century B.C.).

However, opposition to the building was voiced by Jerusalem's neighbors and the building ceased (Chapters 1-4).

In 522 B.C. after the urging of the prophet Haggai and the governor Zechariah, the building of the Temple resumed (Chapters 5-6).

Chapters 7-10, Ezra goes to Jerusalem in 457 B.C. He is a scribe, which means he is a teacher of the Law. With his team he seeks the restoration of the Temple, the command for the

Jews to part from their pagan wives, and the exposition of the Law

---

WHY DID EZRA COMMAND DIVORCE OF PAGAN WIVES?

Ezra lived in the Old Testament Dispensation. God was building a nation of a people from the seed of Abraham who knew God. (Of course a wife born of Pagans, but having faith like Ruth would be an exception)

In the New Testament Paul commands not to divorce the unbelieving spouse, as they may become believers.

NEHEMIAH

Chapters 1-6 tells us of the rebuilding of the walls of Jerusalem. It is debated as to whether these walls had been unrepaired since the captivity or were destroyed since the exiles came back to Jerusalem. (Ezra 9:9 seems to indicate the wall were first repaired under the decree of Cyrus.)

Nehemiah's organization of mobilizing and quickly repairing the walls has been studied by students of management. The walls are rebuilt under the threat and stress of outsiders hostile to the Jews. The workers had to handle a sword as well as a trowel.

Chapters 7-13, Nehemiah and Ezra bring about many moral and spiritual reforms, making Jerusalem a true capital of God's Kingdom.

ESTHER

Chapters 1-4, gives us insight into the life of the exile who remained in pagan lands, particularly the empire of the Medes and Persians. Esther is chosen by the king of Persia to be his wife. An enemy of the Jews in the upper strata of his rule is Haman. He plots to have all Jews in the empire to be annihilated, and tricks king Xerxes I to make such a decree.

Chapters 5-10, Esther risks her life and unannounced goes before the king, inviting him and Haman to a queen's dinner. When the two are in her chambers she reveals she is a Jew and Haman has plotted the extinction of her race.

Haman is hanged, and messengers are dispersed to all of Persia to warn that attacks upon the Jews will have grave consequences from the King.

The Book of Esther never mentions God or prayer (only fasting). It goes out of its way to be silent, so the reader can see that *God has his will or providence in all the deliberations of a sinful human race.*

Secondly, it shows the long reaching effect when a woman of faith takes the risk and uses wisdom to do the Lord's will.

Thirdly, it shows how God prepared the dispersion of the Israelites and their local synagogues to prepare for the coming of the church age, when millions of Gentiles will be brought into the Kingdom.

Finally, the Feast of Purim was initiated by the Jews to celebrate this deliverance by the Lord.

Chapter Seven:
THE POETICAL BOOKS
Job -Song of Songs

The purpose of the poetical book is to teach us God's way with emotion.

JOB is a book with no Hebrew names. It gives no reference to a Temple or of the land of Israel. Its Hebrew vocabulary is, however, like the time of the kings of Israel.

It appears that the life of Job took place among the Gentiles, perhaps during the time of Abraham. It then was orally transmitted through the centuries and then written down by a prophet.

It's ageless lesson schools us how we are to respond to harsh circumstances that fall upon us.

Chapters 1-2, ,the story reveals a dramatic prologue between God and Satan. He accuses Job's devotion to the Lord is due that he has such favorable circumstances. Satan is allow to inflict Job's with awful circumstances in that he loses all his wealth through fire and thievery of the Sebeans of Arabia. Then a hurricane or tornado kills all his sons and daughters.

If that isn't bad enough, Job becomes afflicted by sickness and boils from head to foot.

Here we see that the Devil can be an agent in many troubles that attack us on earth. However, all of it is still under God's will.

Chapters 3-31 ,Job receives terrible advice. first from his wife, who tells him to curse God and die (2:9-10), and then from his ,"friends" who accuse him of sin, which brought about his afflictions, or a poor attitude toward God.

Chapters 32-37, Elihu gives his remarks which seem to defend God. He is the only one of Job's friends who isn't rebuked by God. His speech seems to be an introduction to the Lord's response to Job.

Chapters 38-42, Job meets God, the Lord of creation? In questioning God has Job indulged in putting himself in the place of God? Job responds in true humility and repentance. The Lord vindicates Job before his friends, and charges them to ask Job for forgiveness. Job prays for his friends, and God restores his station in life and more

---

A Christian who suffered a lot put the lesson of Job this way:
    SINCE GOD HAS SHOWN HIS LOVE FOR ME IN WAYS I CAN UNDERSTAND, I WILL TRUST HIM WHEN HE ALLOWS EVENTS I DON'T UNDERSTAND.

What is remarkable about Job is the knowledge he had of God's revelation. He knew he would experience a resurrection from the dead. *I know that my Redeemer lives, and that*

He shall stand at the latter day upon the earth. And though after my skin worms destroy this body, yet in my flesh shall I see God (19:25-26).

If Job lived in Abraham's day, as a believing Gentile, he knew of the second coming of Jesus 2,000 years before it was given in written revelation. He knew of the resurrection of the body, 1500 years before it appeared in the Scriptures.

PSALMS

Hebrew poetry is not like English or European. Our poetry is written with a rhythm:

Mary had a little lamb
Its fleece was white as snow
And everywhere went
The lamb was sure to go

Hebrew poetry is that they take a phrase and *say it again* with different words, or *add to it* or say *the opposite*. These are called *parallelisms*.

For instance:
Bless the Lord, O my soul,
All that is within me, bless His holy Name. (Psalm 103:1)

You see the two phrases state the *same thing*, but in a dramatic variety. It's called a *synthetic parallelism*.

63

Here's another one:
Sing unto Him,
Talk of all his wondrous works
(Psalm 105:2)

Here the parallelism *adds* to the thought, so it called a *progressive parallelism.*

The Lord knows the way of the righteous,
.But the way of the ungodly shall perish (Psalm 1:6).
Here the second phrase is the *opposite* of the first. It's called an *antithetic parallelism.*

The psalms are arranged in five books of 150 psalms. Probably they were gathered when they were composed. Seventy three psalms were written by David. *The heading at the top of the Psalm is part of the work and Scripture.*

There are *Messianic Psalms* which predict Christ, such as Psalm 2 and 110. Others depict an experience that illustrates events in Jesus' life.

> **Read Psalm 22 and see how it describe crucifixion some 800 years before it was practiced.**

PROVERBS

These are 800 short sayings inspired mostly by Solomon. He wrote 3000 proverbs (I Kings 4:32), but incorporated most of his own with some others he considered truths of God. Solomon had a supernatural gift of wisdom (II Chronicles 1:12).

Since Proverbs has 31 chapters, why not take a chapter a day for a month. Write down the proverb that strikes your need and carry it on a card or lip of paper to review that day.

ECCLESIASTES

This book indicates that Solomon became sensible in his old age and followed the wisdom he forsook at the close of his rule. This book makes the point that without God *all is vanity under the sun.*

Chapters 1-6 he shows how human life, history, wisdom and philosophy, religion, achievement, and materialism are empty in themselves.

Chapters 7-12 shows that there is not a just man upon the earth that does good and does not sin (chapter 7:20) He shows certain wise steps in life, but much people seek are not found.

The conclusion of the whole matter: fear God and keep His commandments: for this is the whole duty of man (chapter 12:13).

SOLOMON'S SONG OF SONGS

Here is a celebration of marital love between the king and a gentile woman. It has been called a masterpiece of ancient literature. The Bible does not despise physical love, but teaches that it cannot really be fulfilled, unless it exists within the marriage bond.

Many have seen that since Solomon is a king of Israel, he is a type of Christ and his bride is a type of the church. Spurgeon, the great preacher of the nineteenth century, wrote a 300 page book on the analogy of the Song of Songs and Christ and His church.

Chapter Eight:
THE MAJOR PROPHETS
Isaiah- Daniel

This group of prophetic writings is called *major.* This doesn't mean they are the most important. It only refers to the *length* of the books.

WHEN DID THE PROPHETS WRITE?

DIVIDED KINGS	CAPTIVITY	RETURN
ISAIAH	EZEKIEL	HAGGAI
JEREMIAH	DANIEL	ZECHARIH
HOSEA	OBADIAH	MALACHI
JOEL		
AMOS		
OBADIAH		
JONAH		
MICAH		
NAHUM		
HABAKKUK		
ZEPHANIAH		

If the prophetic book makes no reference to when it was written, then the date has no bearing on the message.

ISAIAH writes of the sins and sinful condition of Israel and Judah..He also prophesies judgment. However, Isaiah has been called the *fifth gospel,* because it contains so many predictions about Christ and His kingdom.

The book was written during the reigns of the kings of Judah, Uzziah, Jotham, Ahaz, and Hezekiah. This was the time of the divided kings, which was one hundred years before the Babylonian Captivity. At that time Assyria was the world power.

Chapters 1-39 make up the first main section of the Book. In it he writes of Judah's great sins and facing judgment. He also writes against the other surrounding nations. Yet, he also writes of the restored glory of Judah and Jerusalem. He speaks of the birth of Emmanuel, (Chapters 7:14; 9:6; 11:1-16) and His glorious Kingdom on earth.

In **Chapters 9-10**, he records the collapse of the Northern Kingdom under Assyria. He conveys the drama of Hezekiah and his faith in standing up to the Assyrians, and subsequent deliverance (Chapter 36-38). Foolishly, Hezekiah entertains a group from Babylonia and shows them the treasures of Judah. Isaiah prophesies the conquering and captivity of Babylon after a 100 years (Chapter 39)

Chapters 40-66 speak of the coming of the Messiah and His rule.The most amazing prophecy is of the Suffering Servant our Lord, where Christ died for our sins. (Chapter 53).

Once a Christian was trying to persuade a very skeptical, Jewish friend about the claims of Jesus Christ.
The Christian began reading from Isaiah 53. "Where do you think I'm reading from?" He asked.
"Oh, from someplace in the New Testament," Answered his friend.
His friend was shocked to see it was a passage written 700 years before Jesus' death. Before long he gave his life to Jesus as his Messiah.

JEREMIAH has been called the *Weeping Prophet,* but he was also the *Persecuted Prophet*

Chapters 1-29, Jeremiah's message warns Judah to submit to the coming Babylonian captivity, as a judgment of God. For this he is persecuted.

Chapters 30-33, Jeremiah next gives prophetic pronouncements of the restoration of Israel (the Northern Kingdom) and Judah. In chapter 33 he predicts the covenant that will bring in the church age.

Mosaic Covenant will be done away. The New Covenant is not like it (v. 32).

God's law will be written on their hearts (v. 33).

All will know the Lord (v.34a)

Jerusalem will remain forever (vv. 35-40).

Chapters 34-39, Jeremiah then gives a history of his opposition and persecution and the fall of Jerusalem,

Chapters 40-52, Finally, Jeremiah gives prophecies of the fate of the nations, and an historical narrative of the captivity and the fate of kings Zedekiah and Jehoiachin.

LAMENTATIONS is written by Jeremiah, where he has obtained the description of the *weeping prophet.*

Chapters 1-5 are a poem of five sections. Each section is built upon the letters of the Hebrew alphabet. It describes the coming sorrows from the assault of Babylon on Jerusalem, the captivity, and a confession and petition for God's mercy.

EZEKIEL writes from the earlier phase of captivity of Babylon

Chapters 1-32, He predicts the Judgments upon Judah and the foreign nations.

Chapters 33-39. In chapter 36:25-28, gives us a description of the new spiritual birth (John 3:3). He removes the heart of stone, makes it a heart of flesh, and puts His Spirit within it.

In chapter 37 he likens spiritually dead Judah to old, dead bones, and predicts a spiritual resurrection which will include a reuniting of Judah and the Northern Kingdom. This whole section speaks of restoration and glories far beyond what occurred when the Jews returned to Judah after the captivity.

Chapters 40-48 are a series of visions depicting a gigantic new Temple (Chapter 40-43) new Priesthood (Chapters 44-46) and new Boundaries of the Land (Chapters 47-48).

While these chapters have similarities to the *customs* of the Mosaic Law, they are different from the requirements of the its *covenant.* 1) the size and location of the Temple, 2) the absence of the holy of holies and the ark of the covenant, 3) the ability for a prince to make sacrifices.

The land will be changed and the Dead Sea will no longer be filled with salt and lifeless. The city for the priests will be 50 square miles, including suburbs (Chapters 47-48).

None of these visions happened when the 50,000 returned to Judah after the captivity. These events have never yet been fulfilled and await another age.

DANIEL divides itself into three sections,

1)**Chapter One** gives us Daniel's early history.

2) **Chapters 2-7**, deals with the times of

the Gentiles.

3) **Chapters 8- 12**, deals with the times of the Gentiles and Israel (Walvoord, *Every Prophecy of the Bible).*

The supernatural source of Daniel is evident in its predictions. Daniel was written over a time of 605-535 B.C. Yet, he predicts nations and events that took place two to four hundred years after he lived

In chapter 2:31-35, 1) Daniel predicted the rise of empires that would follow him to our present. 2) He predicted the details of the rise and fall of Greece, 3) the coming of the Roman Empire and its dissipation as many countries of western civilization. 4) The triumph of God's kingdom. He also predicted events in the New Testament up to 600 years after he died, including the death of the Messiah and the destruction of Jerusalem by the Romans in A.D. 70 (Chapter 9:26).

THE IMAGE THAT DEPICTED THE FIVE EMPIRES OF HISTORY (DANIEL 2:32-35)	
1.HEAD OF GOLD	BABYLON
2.TORSO OF SILVER	MEDO-PERSIA
3.PELVIS OF BRASS	GREECE
4.LEGS OF IRON	ROME
(FEET OF CLAY & IRON	EUROPE & West)
5.ROCK	KINGDOM OFGOD,DESTROYS ALL
THE KINGDOMS, REVELALTION 11: 15	

Chapter Nine:
THE MINOR PROPHETS

HOSEA ministers to the Northern Kingdom (Israel),
Chapters 1-3 warns them to repent of their sins or face coming judgment. This is illustrated by the unfaithfulness of his wife and her eventual restoration.
Chapters 4-14 cites their sins and their impending judgment and exil .He ends by predicting Israel's repentance and restoration.

JOEL speaks of famine and the Day of the Lord,

Chapters 1-2 tells of a great invasion of locusts, which is likened to the *Day of the Lord* which is to follow. Here we comprehend that this phrase used in the Old and New Testaments speaks of a time of *Judgment and Punishment followed by a time of blessing.* Also he calsl for repentance and blessing that can follow. He speaks of the pouring out of the Holy Spirit *upon all flesh* (2:28-29).

Chapter 3 speaks of the judgment upon all nations and the everlasting preservation of Israel.

Peter at Pentecost spoke that the pouring out of the Holy Spirit prophesied in Joel was then being fulfilled (Acts 2:16-18). He then quotes Joel 2:30-31, which speaks of coming judgment. This we see fulfilled in Revelation, where God's wrath is poured out on earth

However, he also quotes Joel 2:32, *whosoever will call upon the name of the Lord will be saved.* (Paul uses this same invitation in Romans 10:13).

AMOS, a farmer who comes from Judah, is sent by God as a prophet to preach to the Northern Kingdom, Israel.

Chapters 1-4 announces the coming judgment of God on all the surrounding nations, ending with Israel.

Chapters 5-6 describe the Assyrian Captivity.

Chapters 7-9 are seven visions of judgment and restoration: 1) Vision of Locusts (Assyrian army), 2) Vision of Fire, 3) Vision of the Plumbline (Israel is measured and found off God's standard), 4) The Judgment upon Amaziah the Priest, 5) Vision of Spoiling Summer Fruit, 6) Vision of the Altar's Destructon, 7) The Raising Up of David's Tent(dwelling and rule) and Prosperity in the Land.

This prosperity will include the Gentiles or heathen *which are called by my name.* James uses this passage of God's inclusion of Gentiles in the future kingdom to justify that Gentiles can come into the church as Gentiles (Acts 15:17-18)
.

OBADIAH speaks of Edom's Judgment.

Edom was founded by Jacob's brother Esau. It also promises that Israel will posses its borders. When the Romans took over Judea they made Herod the Great the kings. He was an Edomite, as were his sons who ruled after him. Evenutally, the Edomites were absorbed into the tribe of Juda

JONAH is one of the most famous prophets of the Old Testament.

Chapter One tells of his call to preach to Nineveh, the capital of Assyria. Jonah so hated the Assyrian, he seeks to escape by a ship to Tarshish. In a storm Jonah is thrown overboard and swallowed by a great fish, prepared by the Lord (possibly a whale.).

Chapter Two Jonah prays inside the belly of the whale and it vomits him onto the shore.

Chapter Three, Jonah preaches to the people of Nineveh, and to his dislike they repent and turn to God.

Chapter Four, Noah is sitting and pouting under a gourd's shade, but at night a worm kills it. As he complains about the gourd, the Lord answers, that Jonah found pleasure in a plant he didn't make. How much more should God take pleasure and spare 120,000 people, who *cannot discern between their left hand and their right* *hand,* and their animals. The lesson of Jonah is that *we are to love our enemies and pray for their salvation, as our Lord taught.*

I once heard Dr. Alan Redpath of Moody Church give a series on Jonah at Columbia International University. In his research he found that sperm whales can become sick from a fungal infection, which widens their throat, allowing all kinds of objects to enter. They eventually die.

A nineteenth century newspaper reported that a whaler cut open a fresh catch and found one of his crew alive inside the stomach. The face and hands were bleached white from the remains of stomach acid. Imagine the horror of the Ninevites, seeing Noah with such an appearance!

MICAH speaks of God's dissatisfaction of the wickedness of the Northern and Southern Kingdoms.

Chapter One reveals God's judgment: the destruction of the Northern Kingdom under Assyria. The Assyrians will destroy her.

Chapters 2-7 speaks of the sins of Israel, but also of the triumph of the coming Messiah and His rule. The Lord will have mercy as He promised to Abraham and Jacob.

NAHUM is a short book predicting the destruction of Assyria.

Chapters 1-3. Though God used Assyria as the *rod of His anger*, they will meet judgment.

The Assyrians would often lead their captives with nose-hooks, or kill them by impaling.

HABAKKUK

Chapter 1 the prophet has difficulty with God's ways. His first problem is 1) Why Does God overlook the indifference to Him by Judah and their sin. 2) When they are judged, why does God use the Babylonians, who are more wicked than Judah?

Chapter 2 God answers the second question in that He will punish the Babylonians in the future..

Chapter 3 Habakkuk sees a vision of the majesty of God and declares he will rejoice in the God of His salvation.

ZEPHANIAH ministered during the rule of King Josiah, the godly king who sought to reverse the policies of the wicked king Manasseh.

In **Chapters 1-2** he prophesies judgment upon the Gentile nations.

Chapter 3, Speaks of judgment on Jerusalem, but there will be a purification of its remnant. However, the Lord promises to reestablish Jerusalem after the captivity.

HAGGAI ministered to the people who returned to Jerusalem after the Babylonian captivity. Because of opposition they stopped rebuilding the Temple for 16 years. Instead they built and maintained good houses for themselves.

In **Chapter 1**, during the fall of 520 B.C., Haggai rebukes the population for their failure, and gets an enthusiastic response.

Chapter 2, he encourages them, and prophesies of the overthrow of the Gentile kingdoms and that the Lord's city is the chosen of the Lord.

ZECHARIAH seems to have written this prophecy when the Greeks had become a world-wide empire, defeating the Persians.

Chapters 1-8. He speaks to those finishing the Temple calling for repentance, but also gives eight visions speaking of Israel's coming prosperity

Chapters 9-14 speak of the Messiah and His coming Kingdom. At first Israel will reject Him. Afterward, the Lord will **pour out a spirit of grace and supplication, and they shall look upon me, whom they have pierced, and they shall mourn for Him** (Chapter 12:10).

This conversion to Christ will be costly, for two thirds of the Israelites will be killed (13:8). However in Chapter 14, the Day of the Lord will commence, and He will battle the nations. The end results will be that all the nations will go to Jerusalem io *the King, the Lord of Hosts* (the armies of heaven.) Much of this, it seems, will be fulfilled in Revelation 19-20.

Zechariah also illustrates that the term *Day of the Lord* speaks of Judgment followed by His plan of grace and victory (Joel 2:11; Zephaniah 2:3; Zechariah 14:1; and I Thessalonians 5:2).

MALACHI seems to have ministered after the passing of Haggai and Zechariah, around 430 B.C.

Chapters 1 speaks of God's love for Israel, against the corruption of the priests,

Chapter 2 condemns the prevalence of divorce and marriage to unbelieving heathen,

Chapter 3 condemns the neglect of tithes and offerings for the Lord.

Chapter 4 promises the coming of the Lord to vanquish the wicked. Yet, to those that fear the Lord, *Sun of righteousness will arise with healing in His wings* (Malachi 4:2)

THE MAJOR COVENANTS

We cannot really understand the Bible unless we understand these covenants

---

EDENIC , TEMPORARY (Genesis 2:17. Hosea 6:7) This covenant was made with Adam and Eve, who disobeyed and plunged the human race and the planet under the curse.

NOAHIC, PERMANENT (Genesis 9:1-18) This Covenant was made with Noah and his family, to carry out filling the earth with offspring, to eat animal protein, to exact capital punishment for murder, as all humans are made in God's image.

ABRAHAMIC, PERMANENT (Genesis 12-17; 17:7). This Covenant was made with Abraham to bring about a people, a nation, and land. The world-wide blessing culminates in Jesus Christ.

MOSAIC , TEMPORARY (Exodus 20; Jeremiah 31:31.) This Covenant regulated Israel and taught them their need for grace and atonement.

DAVIDIC, PERMANENT (II Samuel 2 & Psalm 89) A descendent will be on Israel's throne forever, fulfilled in Jesus.

NEW, PERMANENT (Jeremiah 31:31-40; Hebrews 13:20) This Covenant puts God's law in our hearts and all within it, know the Lord. It is this Covenant in which the church of Jesus operates.

Chapter Ten:
THE GOSPELS AND ACTS

The Gospels are more than just histories of the ministry of Jesus. Each Gospel has a unique emphasis about His life and ministry.

MATTHEW emphasizes that Jesus is the **Son of David**, and heir to the Davidic Covenant Kingship.

Chapters 1-4, records the birth, preparation and beginnings of Jesus' earthly ministry.Interestingly, Matthew gives Jesus' royal genealogy, and includes the names of four women. Tamar, who bore a son to Judah as a Prostitute;, Rahab and Ruth, who were Gentiles; and Bathsheba, who committed adultery with King David. It shows that God overcomes sin and defeat and carries on His will in grace.

Chapters 5-25 give the ministry and particularly the teachings of Jesus

Chapters 26-28 relate the death, resurrection and Great Commission of Jesus. All four gospels give the commission, but Matthew's version is more detailed.

MARK, who history tells us wrote under the authority of Peter. This gospel, the shortest of the four, emphasizes Jesus as the **Miraculous Servant.**

Chapters 1-13 concentrate on Jesus' northern ministry in Galilee and beyond Galilee. It then ends with Jesus' ministry in the south in Judea and Jerusalem. Mark emphasizes the tremendous activity of His public ministry. A key phrase repeated over and over is *and it came to pass.*

Chapters 14-16 finish with the death, resurrection and great commission of Jesus.

LUKE, as an historian addresses his gospel to a Theophilus and takes up the birth and ministry of Jesus. Written under the authority of Paul, he appeals to Gentile readers. Yet, his recording of the birth of Jesus is the most "Jewish" part of the New Testament. Luke depicts Jesus as the **Son of Man,** the One who comes to save Gentiles as well as Jews.

Chapters 1-3 reveal the birth of John the Baptist and Jesus, his cousin. In this passage are the strongest declaration of Jesus as the fulfillment of the Davidic Covenant.

Chapters 4-21 concentrate on Jesus' Galilean ministry, his ministry traveling to Jerusalem, and His ministry in that holy city.

Chapters 22-24 pin point the death and resurrection of Jesus, and particularly how He showed the fulfillment of His ministry through the Old Testament predictions.

These three Gospels are connected because they emphasize the three year ministry of Jesus and the events of His life.

JOHN'S GOSPEL is unique. It is obvious that he knows the content of the other Gospels, and supplies information not revealed in them. John spends half of the Gospel on the last week of Jesus' ministry: His personal teaching to His disciples, His crucifixion, and resurrection. As an eye-witness, he gives some graphic details of Jesus death. The emphasis about Jesus in this Gospel is the **deity of Jesus, as the Son of God.**

The two most famous verses come out of Jesus' talk with Nicodemus.

You must be born again (John 3:3)

For God so loved the world that He gave His only begotten Son, that whosoever believeth in Him should not perish, but have everlasting life (John 3:16).

Chapter 1 begins with a prologue of His background from eternity as God, and His incarnation to bring grace and truth, and to reveal the invisible God (1:1-18). The rest of the chapter speaks of His baptism under John the Baptist, and His earlier acquaintance with those whom He would call to be His disciples.

Chapters 2-11 give his various discourses and miraculous signs that He is the Son of God. 1) Turning water into wine (2:1-12). 2) Healing of the nobleman's son (4:43-54). 3) Healing of the paralytic (5:1-47). 4) The feeding of the 5000 (6:1-71). 5) Walking on water (6:16-21). 7) The raising of Lazarus from the dead (11:1-15). Of course Jesus performed many more miracles than these (John 21:25). These, however, are singled out by John to show His evidence as the Son of God.

Chapters 12-20 give Jesus' private ministry to His eleven disciples. Here is the climax of God's revelation in His earthly ministry. *Progressive interpretation means that you take all of the teachings of the other three gospels and add to them the final words of our Lord.* One example: Our Lord teaches us to pray in Matthew 6:9-15 and Luke 11:1-13. However, further revelation by Jesus tells us to pray in His name (His authority and mediatorship), John 14:13-14.

Chapter 21 is the postscript of the book, probably written after John wrote Chapters 1-20. Here we read of the restoration of the disciples, including Peter, and His fate as the Lord's follower. It also shows that John would live on. He lived a long life and wasn't martyred.

ACTS is the second book written by Luke, the physician, under the authority of Paul. Like his gospel, it is addressed to Theophilus. Acts can be divided roughly into two parts:

, **Chapters 1-12** the ministry and influence of Peter.

Chapters 13-28 Paul becomes the prominent figure in the last half of the book,. He was converted to Christ when He saw the risen Jesus in blazing light on his way to Damascus. His companions saw the light, heard a voice speaking to Paul, but didn't hear the words. He fulfilled Jesus mission to carry His name to Gentiles, kings, and chiLdren of Israel (9:15). This section records the three missionary journeys (Chapters 13-14; 15-18:22; and 18:23-21:16) and ends with his journey to Rome (21:17-28).

WATER BAPTISM IN THE GOSPELS AND ACTS

In the Gospels we have many responding to John the Baptist by being baptized, confessing their sins (Matthew 3:6). However, baptism didn't cleanse from sin, but was a confession of repentance. When several from the religious establishment wanted to be baptized, John requires that they give evidence of repentance. In other words baptism didn't give grace. It was the *testimony* of grace.

In Acts 2:38, Peter declares *Repent and be baptized every one of you in the name of Jesus for the remission of sins.* The little word *for* means *because* not *cause.* The Greek word translated *for* is the word meaning *unto* or *in reference to.* No ritual can save anyone. Millions are relying on the ritual of baptism to be saved. However, true faith is the only link to God's saving grace. Baptism is only a picture of salvation.

BAPTISM IN THE SPIRIT

Jesus tells the disciples to wait in Jerusalem for the baptism in the Spirit (Acts 1:5,). When Pentecost came, the `120 disciples were gathered in the upper room and tongues of fire came upon them. They began to speak in other tongues and the people from all over the surrounding countries heard them speak in their own native languages. This gave outward proof of the new entity of the New Testament Church. The sign of other languages supernaturally given, duplicated the events of Pentecost. This demonstrated that all the following groups were brought into the body of Christ (I Corinthians 12:13).

First the Jews, Acts 2:1-4

Secondly, the Samarians, Acts 8:16-17

Thirdly, the Gentiles, Acts 10:45-46

Fourthly, the Disciples of John the Baptist. They had only an Old Testament understanding of the faith, and had never heard there was a Holy Spirit (Acts 19:1-7).

Acts concludes with the author , Luke, the Gentile doctor, accompanying Paul. When they were shipwrecked, Luke observed first-hand the miracle healings of the population in Melita (Acts 27:4,5,7; 28:11.13,14).

Sir William Ramsey believed Luke's writings were preposterous. He set out to disprove him by looking at ancient historical documents, traveling where Luke said he traveled, and archeology.

Ramsey concluded that <u>Luke was the greatest historian ever</u>! On Luke's testimony he became a Christian and the father of New Testament archeology.

Chapter Eleven:
PAUL'S LETTERS:
Romans

ROMANS is a letter written by the Apostle Paul, which systematically lays out what the early apostles proclaimed throughout the world.

Chapters 1-3:20, tells the *great need* for the message of grace.

Chapter One speaks of the *Gentile* world under God's wrath. This wrath is that the Lord allows them to walk away from the spiritual light of God and reap the results of a corrupt and immoral society.

Chapter Two demonstrates that the *Jewish* world are sinners even thought they have God's law and are subject of God's wrath as well. While the first two chapters speak of the general *extensive* need for grace, Chapter 3:10-20 focuses in on our *inward* condition as sinners, deserving God's wrath.

We all need desperately the good news of God's Grace. We can only receive grace and salvation through faith in Jesus Christ. He died and took on Himself the wrath of God for all sin.

(Romans 3:25). Jesus met the penalty of the Law for all who will truly believe on Him.

Chapters 4-5 reveals that the only way anyone can be reconciled to God is by faith alone and not by our works.

This is demonstrated by Abraham and David (4:3-6). God gave us Jesus who laid down His life in His great love for us as sinners (Chapter 4). Paul then spells out that the first human (Adam) represented the human race when he plunged us into sin by His disobedience. Now our Lord, who kept the law perfectly, died for us as our representative on the cross. His obedience to die brought freedom from condemnation to all who believe (Chapter 5).

In **Chapters 6-11** Paul answers objections to the gospel.

Chapter 6 answers the question, *"Does the Gospel lead to sin, since we are saved by faith alone and not of our works?*

Paul establishes that we are united to Christ and have died to the slavery of sin. We are to *know* that we died with Christ and rose with Him. Therefore, we are not longer under the domain of sin (6:1-10).

We must then *reckon (consider)* that we are dead to sin and alive to God through Jesus Christ (v.11). *Sin shall not have any dominion over you; for you are not under law but under grace* (v, 14).

Our relationship to Jesus dictates to us, *yield your members slaves to righteousness unto holiness* (v. 19).

Our relationship with Christ in grace brings us to a vital life of holiness and at the end of life, everlasting life. *For the wages of sin is death, but the gift of God is eternal life through Jesus Christ our Lord* (vv. 20-23).

Therefore the gospel saves us not by works, but as a free gift. When we receive Christ by faith, we have a new relationship with Him, and are no longer slaves to sin. Therefore , we know our position, and yield ourselves to Him and holiness.

Chapters 7-8 answer the question about the law (of Moses).

Since we died with Christ, we are delivered from the Law's condemnation (7:6). Paul then tells us of his experience before he became a Christian, *when the commandment came, sin revived, and I died* (7:9). The law's function was to show us our sin and need for holiness. *The law is holy, just and good* (7:12).

He then tells us his experience with the law as a Christian. The commands only bring conflict. *For what I would, that I do not* (neglect God's will). *But what I hate* (transgress God's will) *that do I* (7:15). This shows that any teaching of just morality will fail because of our sinful makeup.

Paul cries out about the sinfulness dwelling within him, *O wretche man that I am, who will deliver me from the body of this death?* (7:24).

The wonderful answer, *I thank God through Jesus Christ our Lord* (7:25).

This is further answered by **Chapter 8.** There is *no condemnation* in Christ. The *law of the Spirit* makes us free from the *law of sin and death* (**Chapter 8:1-2**). The law's righteous standard is fulfilled as we walk in the Spirit. We do not live a life dictated by the fallen nature, because the Spirit of God dwells in us. The power of the Spirit that raise Jesus from the dead, enables us to *put to death the deeds of the body.* It is the Spirit of God that assures us by

His *witness with our spirit that we are the children of God* (8:4-17).

No matter how we may suffer, nothing in this world compares to what awaits us with glory which will be revealed in us. This is also true of the world, which is subject to corruption (due to the fall). It will be delivered from its bondage. Creation and the Holy Spirit within us wait for the *redemption of our body* (vv. 21-27).

This security is also demonstrated in that with God *all things work together for good to them that love God.*(v. 28). This good is our being conformed to Jesus Christ (v. 29).

God has purposed and sovereignly fixed our journey through life. Paul used a Greek verb which speaks of action accomplished, *.Predestinated...called...justified...glorified* (v 30). Glorified takes place when we are resurrected. Why is it described as already taken place? Because in the purpose of God, we, who are justified (declared righteous by Christ's death and resurrection) are secured a place with the Lord. Our journey to that time is assured because we are not under law, but under grace.

Chapters 9-11 answer the problem why so few Jews receive Jesus as their Messiah.

Chapter 9 informs us that only a remnant were included in Israel, according to God's election. It was only through Abraham's son Isaac that Abraham's seed would be called into the kingdom (vv. 6-8),

When Rebekah bore twins, only the younger, Jacob, not Esau would be the heir. So according to election, not works, *the elder shall serve the younger.*

Now the next verse has been a shocker for many, so we need to give a longer explanation.

As it is written, Jacob have I loved, but Esau have I hated (v. 13, quotes Malachi 1:3). Does this mean that God hated Esau before he was even born? Some have so taught. However, when you find a hard to understand passage, look up what faithful teachers have found, and "put it on the back burner" until you find an adequate answer. What I am going to give you took me some 45 years. (I actually found the answer in a book about Hebrew word studies.)

1) Does God hate? Hatred is sin (Psalm 34:21; Galatians, 5:10), and God cannot sin. The word means to be *zealously against.* In other words it means being under God's strong disfavor.

2) When did God say He was strongly against Esau? In Malachi 1:3, about 1500 years after Esau lived. *I hated Esau and his mountains and inheritance waste.* Edom was conquered by Esau, who despised his birthright and the country became an enemy of Israel. The land had become a *border of wickedness* (v. 4)

3) The context is clear. In the womb God chose Jacob, not Esau, to be in the line of Abraham and developer of Israel. Esau, who despised his birthright, conquered Edom and lived there. This land then grew eventually as a place of wickedness and became eventually under God's disfavor.

Chapter 10 tells us that though it was God's plan to save a remnant (*I will have mercy upon those whom I will have mercy*, 9:15) *those not included in the remnant of believers have themselves to blame.* They sought to be saved by their works not by faith alone in God's mercy.

It's only by faith that we are reconciled to God. Therefore we need to send people to give the message, Confess the Lord Jesus, believe in your heart that God raised Him from the dead.

For whosoever calls upon the name of the Lord will be saved (10:6-13).

Chapter 11 reveals that someday the full number of Gentiles will be brought into the Kingdom. Then the whole nation of Israel will turn to the Lord and be saved (v.26).

Chapters 12-16 Paul tells us we need always be a living sacrifice for the Lord (Romans 12:1-2). We need to exercise in love the gifts given to us for the benefit of others in the congregation. We also need to put ourselves out to help in love even for our enemies (12:3-21). We should be respectful and honor all authorities, and give honor and taxes due to them (13:1-7). We need to be careful not to be a stumbling block in exercising our Christian liberties (14:1-23). In Chapter 15 Paul gives his great vision to reach more and more Gentiles for Christ. Chapter 16 is filled with personal greeting for many who have served with him, who are now in Rome.

Here's an Easy Project
We need to send communications to those whom we have known in the Lord.
A card, phone call, or an email may just be the right encouragement for someone today.

Chapter Twelve:
More of PAUL'S LETTERS:
I Corinthians - Ephesians

I CORINTHIANS is the great problem-solver for church difficulties.

Chapter 1 deals with divisions and true service in the congregation. Essentially, we are not to be groupies for one personality over another. All are given to us to advance the Lord's kingdom.

Chapter 2 Paul talks about sowing, Apollos watering, and God giving the increase. Paul speaks of how God gives the truth to spokesmen like the Apostle.

Chapter 3 charges that the Corinthians were acting like unbelievers the way they were conducting the affairs to the church. He then warns that he laid the foundation of Christ for the church. Any ministries laid on that foundation will be evaluated like a burning fire. Superficial, prideful, or divisive efforts will be burned up, yet they will be saved, yet through the scourging test of our service for the Lord.

WE NEED TO SELF-EVALUATE OUR SERVICE DAILY

It's easy to fall into serving the Lord for the applause of others. Do we get peeved when we're not noticed or thanked? Do we get jealous because someone is asked instead of us? We need daily to refocus and serve the Lord alone, regardless of how people act.

What's worst is when we hide the truth or ignore it in order to please people and not the Lord. Whole ministries have been build on entertaining and only tell people what they want to hear. Ministries have been focused on self-promotion. How sad when like "hay, wood, and stubble" God's servants will see that their efforts were worthless to the Lord.

What a tragedy to serve the Lord for a life-time, and see all the effort "go up in smoke." Saved, yet so "as by fire" (I Corinthians 4:15).

Chapters 5-6 speaks to church discipline and excommunication. In my observation I've found two extremes: 1) it is never carried out, the majority of cases, or 2) it is carried out too hastily and without proper investigation. In all such cases there are three stages. Please study carefully **Matthew 18:15-17** Also, remember that the attitude in dealing with the erring brother or sister is **Galatians 6:1.**

In **Chapter 5** Paul speaks that he or any church official havr no authority in the world. On the hand, no worldly authority should have authority in the local church. **Chapter 6** states, no Christian should take his brother in the congregation to court. Such matters should be deliberated within the church. Here we see that *the State is separated from the Church and the Church is separated from the state.*

Chapter 7 speaks of marriage, where the Apostle tells that sexual relations should not be neglected. Also, he delights in the service he can render as single, and it may be good for many because of the *present distress* (v. 26), **However,** this is not prohibition to marriage, except it must be *in the Lord* (v. 39). However, if a believer has an unbelieving spouse, the believer is to live with the spouse, as they are under special influence with a believer in the home.

Chapters 8-10 speaks to sensitivity about buying the bargain meat that was once offered to an idol. If that is interpreted by a weaker believer that the Christian is indulging in idolatry, then that Christian should not buy or eat the meat in front of the weaker believer.

Chapter 11 is instructive of public meetings of the church. Women should dress modestly and not like men in the public assembly. In observing Communion we are to be conscious of all the brethren, and not withdraw from those who are poor or of low station in life.

Paul instructs us that the bread and cup is a *communion with the Lord* (I Corinthians 10:16). Moreover, Communion is to be taken together (11:17), as a *remembrance* of the Lord's death. In this *ye show the Lord's death until He come* (v.26). Communion speaks of the cross of Jesus, the great equalizer for us all.

> **Before we take communion let's resolve: to forgive anyone who has wronged us; to clear up any issued we might have with other brethren; to be more loving and aware of those who have needs in our congregation.**

Chapters 12-14 speaks of the spiritual gifts and especially the gift of tongues. In *Chapter 12:13* Paul writes that all believer are baptized in the Spirit, but all do not speak in tongues (vv. 7-11). It is the Spirit's will how He distributes the gifts. Some of the gifts are supernatural, other (administration and helps) are natural made supernatural for the ministry to the body of Christ. In **Chapter 13** in the most famous chapter of this Book, Paul speaks of the importance of love and how it is to be practiced. He concludes that love is greater than any gift and last longer than *faith* and *hope,* because someday we will see what we believe and hope for, but love continues forever. **Chapter 14** concludes that in the public assembly of the church all tongues must be interpreted and only up to three prophets are to speak. Paul is conscious that he writes and speaks the commandment of God given directly to him by the Holy Spirit (v.37).

Chapter 15 gives us one of the great evidences of the resurrection. Paul not only lists those who saw the risen Lord, but is able to produce 500 witnesses together who saw Him risen. These were witnesses who are honest, faithful, and willing to be put to death for their testimony.

In Chapter 15 Paul is refuting the idea by some Corinthians, while believing that Jesus rose from the dead bodily, did   not think Christians would likewise be raised. Paul shows the inconsistency of this and explains the nature of our resurrected bodies. Finally he conveys the mystery of the believer's resurrection. (A *mystery* is revealed truth never before given.)   This mystery is that not only dead believers will be resurrected, but those living will also be resurrected when the Lord comes back (vv. 51-58).

Chapter 16 concludes with instructions for an offering he will take up for the relief of those in Jerusalem.   He then gives personal instructions and greetings to several families and individuals at Corinth.

II CORINTHIANS contains much insight into the heart of Paul.

Chapters 1-2 are a defense why he could not come and visit Corinth, though he told them he wanted to come. Apparently, this was being used to undermine his authority as an Apostle. He also tells them to receive the individual who was disciplined and excommunicated in I Corinthians 5. He had repented, but lack of comforting him might result in his being *swallowed up with overmuch sorrow* (v. 7).

Chapter 3 describes the effect of the New Covenant in ministry. The Holy Spirit lifts a veil over minds so people can understand the Scriptures and be changed. The Holy Spirit is the the Lord (God) and changes us from glory to glory.

Chapters 4-7 Paul explains his ministry of reconciliation to the world, and what should be their response to him and his ministry.

Chapters 8-9 speak of the coming offering that the Corinthians promised to give to the needy. In this section are great teaching of our responsibilities in giving.

Chapter 10-11 reestablish his apostolic authority and his dealing with sin when he comes.

GALATIANS warns against those who would undermine the Gospel of grace.

Chapters 1-2 Paul cites that after his conversion he was given the truth of God independently of the other apostles. He was received by *James, Peter, and John* called *pillars of the church* (of Jerusalem). They testified that what Paul taught was exactly what was given to them by Jesus and the Holy Spirit.

However, men from Jerusalem came to Antioch insisting that Gentile converts needed to be circumcised and keep the Law of Moses. Peter, who had been eating with the Gentiles, then withdrew when these men came and only ate food required by the Law. Paul rebuked Peter openly, accusing him of hypocrisy (2:11-14). This showed that Peter's action was not because he disagreed with Paul that Gentile believers were not subject to Mosaic Law. Peter had acted hypocritically (vv. 13-14).

Chapters 2:15-3:18 explain that we were redeemed from the Law by Christ's death for us, Grace comes only through faith, as Abraham believed *and it was accounted to him for righteousness* (3:6).

Because of faith alone we are made children of Abraham, not by the Law. Furthermore all divisions spiritually are removed between Jew and Gentile, slave and free,or male and female (3:19-20).

Chapter 4 declares that the true spiritual purpose of the Law was to teach us to come to Christ. Now that the Law had accomplished its purpose, we are to cast out the Mosaic Law as Abraham cast out Hagar (Sarah's servant and son).

Chapters 5-6 then tell us that since we have been made free by Christ, do not become *entangled again with the yoke of bondage* of the Mosaic Law (5:1).

However, we are not to use this freedom *as an occasion of the flesh* (*sinful makeup,* 5:13). If we *walk in the Spirit,* we'll *not fulfill the lust of the flesh* (v.16). There is a warfare between the flesh (sinful nature) and the Spirit of God. In ourselves we cannot do what we would. However, we must surrender to the leading of the Spirit in holiness. In doing that we are free from the defeat of resolutions and the law which cannot deliver.

On the positive side the *fruit of the Spirit* produces in us *love, joy, peace, long-suffering, gentleness, goodness, faith, meekness* (no resistance to God's will, sometimes translated *gentleness), temperance* (5:22-23).

A GREAT SPIRITUAL PROJECT FOR US ALL

Take Galatians 5:22-23 as a memory verse for the week. Write it down on a paper or keep it in your cell phone. Periodically, every day go over the verse and then reflect on each characteristic.

Keep track of any times of failure to exhibit these characteristics and ask the Lord for help. Then watch how the Lord begins to work these aspects of His fruit in us each day.

EPHESIANS

Chapter 1, with a praise for God the Father's salvation in His choosing us, the Son's work in our redemption, and the Holy Spirit's ministry of sealing us as a guarantee of our future salvation,(vv. 1-14). Paul then prays that the Ephesian Christians will be given wisdom and revelation to know the great calling and destiny of their inheritance in Christ. He wants them to experience the power that is available to us. This was given to Jesus, when He was raised from the dead (vv. 15-23).

Chapter 2 spells out our salvation is by grace through faith. We were once dead in sin and lived under the control of the Devil and the desires of the world and our fallen nature. However, God in His rich mercy saved us and made us spiritually alive in Christ by His grace (vv. 1-7).

For by grace are you saved through faith and that not of yourselves. It is the gift of God, not of works, lest any man should boast.

For we are His workmanship, created in Christ Jesus to good works, that God has before ordained that we should walk in them (2:8-10).

> This is a great passage to memorize, not only for our own assurance, but a wonderful explanation of how anyone can be saved.

Paul then shows that now the Lord has taken the Jew and the Gentile and made them one in a new body. We are now fellow citizens with the saints and the household of God. We are being built up in Christ as a holy temple in the Lord. This is all done by the work of the Holy Spirit (vv. 11-22).

Chapter 3 sets forth Paul's ministry to minister among the Gentiles that they by the Lord's effectual working in power see the riches of Christ. He is proclaiming a former *mystery*, which was not revealed in the Old Testament. It is the truth of the church, which is His eternal purpose in Christ.

Chapter 4 reveals the unity of the Spirit, which we have. We only need to keep it. The Lord gave the teaching gifts so that while we are one in the Spirit, we will grow to be unified in our knowledge of the faith (vv.1-13)

Therefore, we are to live and grow up spiritually, speaking the truth in love. Like shedding old, filthy garments and putting on clean clothing, we have *put off* the old life and have *put on Christ* (vv. 14-22).

So we are to keep putting off the old patterns of our past life, and replace them with those patterns consistent with our new life in Christ.
Paul then list several sins and how they are to be replaced by consistent patterns of life (vv. 23-32).

Grieve not the Holy Spirit of God, whereby you were sealed to the day of redemption (v. 30).

Chapters 5-6 then command us to walk in love as Christ has loved us (5:1-20) He then tells us to submit to one another (v. 21), and introduces how we are to live as 1) husband and wife (vv. 22-33); 2) children and parents (6:1-4); 3) Christian slaves and masters (6:1-9).

Finally, he shows us how to be *strong in the Lord* by putting on God's armor (6:10-18). 1) feet shod with the gospel; 2) taking the shield of faith; 3) the helmet of salvation; 4) the sword of the Spirit; 5) praying always.

PHILIPPIANS probably was written during Paul's first imprisonment in Rome.

Chapter 1 Paul writes of his appreciation for this congregation and security in Christ. *He that began a good work in you will perform it* (bring it to completeness) *until the Day of Jesus Christ* (v.6).

His imprisonment has led to the *furtherance of the gospel* (v. 12). This has encouraged others to share the gospel (vv.14-17).

Paul speaks of our confidence after death. *For to me to live is Christ but to die is gain* (v. 21). While he would rather be in heaven than in prison, he knows that this is best for his ministry of helping their faith grow (vv. 21-30).

Chapter 2 commands us to have the *mind of Christ* (v. 5). The ultimate of servanthood is seen in Christ's example. 1) What He turned from: Being in the very *form of God,* He did not hold on to His position of being *equal with God* (v. 6). 2) What He became: **made Himself of no reputation, became a man, humbled Himself, and became obedient to the death of the cross** (vv. 7-8). Therefore the incarnate Son of God is exalted above all names and all creation on earth and heaven (vv. 9-11).

Because God is working in us to the very end (v. 13), we are to be blameless servants, *holding forth the word of life* (vv. 15-18).

Chapter 3 give warning about false teaching. There were the *false legalists* who wanted to put Gentile Christians under the law of Moses (contrary to Acts 15). Paul tells of his background as a Pharisee of the Pharisees (the strictest sect of the Jews) and regards his legalistic status as garbage (vv. 1-8). He now has his righteousness by faith in Christ, not righteousness according to the Law of Moses. This causes him to seek the experiential l knowledge of Christ, His power and the *fellowship of his suffering* (vv. 9-10). So all of us are by experience to *press toward the mark of the prize of the high calling of God in Christ Jesus* (vv. 11-15).

The other false teaching is giving mental assent to God's grace, but continuing to walk in sin and focus on the sinful pleasures of the world (vv. 18-21).

Chapter 4 we are given practical steps to possessing peace. We are to make it a habit to *rejoice in the Lord* and live a moderate life (vv.4-5). Do not be filled with cares, but take everything to the Lord in prayer and thanksgiving making known your requests to the Lord. By such patterns of life we will receive the peace of God *that passes all understanding* (vv. 4-7). Fill our minds with good and virtuous thoughts and practice what the godly teach and model for us. (vv. 8-9). Learn the lessons of being content with little or much. We can do this through Christ, who *strengthens us* (vv. 10-13). Finally, be aware of God's promise, *God shall supply all your needs according to His riches in glory by Christ Jesus* (v. 19).

Chapter Thirteen:
PAUL'S LETTERS:
Colossians- Titus

COLOSSIANS has many of the themes of Ephesians but in shortened forms.

Chapter 1 speaks of the preeminence of Christ is all things. We have redemption and forgiveness of our sins because of His shed blood. Jesus is *the image of the invisible God* through His incarnation and *the firstborn of every creature,* meaning He inherits all creation as the virgin-born Son of Man. He created all things. He is before all things. And all things are held together by Him. (vv. 14-19.)

Paul then serves the Lord by bringing reconciliation of God with the Gentiles. This is because of Jesus' death (vv. 20-22). He proclaims the mystery that was never revealed before of *Christ in you the hope of glory* (vv. 21-29).

Chapter 2 commands us that *as you have received Christ Jesus the Lord, so walk you in Him* (v. 5). As we become *rooted and grounded in Him*, we are to be free from false legalisms like dietary laws or judging anyone about keeping Sabbath days.

Chapter 3 shows us how to live the Christian life. We're to set our affections on things above (v.3); putting off the old way of life, and putting on daily the new life in Christ (vv. 8-

10). We are to *let the word of Christ dwell in you richly in all wisdom, teaching, and admonitions one another in psalms, and hymns, and spiritual songs* (vv. 16). Interestingly, Ephesians 6:18-19 has almost the same wording except Paul states that we are to *be being filled with the Spirit. Obviously, being continually filled with the Spirit is allowing the word of God to dwell in us richly.*

Chapter 3 ends like with the same exhortations of Ephesians 4. Wives submit to their husbands, and husbands love their wives. Children obey their parents, but fathers are not to provoke them to discouragement. Slaves serve heartily the Lord in their work.

Chapter 4:1 finishes the thought that Masters are to give to those under them what is just and fair. The rest of the chapter deals with living consistently not only among Christians but those in the world (vv. 2-6). The letter concludes with greetings.

SLAVERY AND THE BIBLE

In the Old Testament slaves were voluntary servants, who agreed to serve for no more than seven years at a time. A better translation would be "servants" as the King James renders it.

In the New Testament the Empire of Rome had more slaves than citizens. Slavery was undermined by the church, as all masters and slaves were brothers and sisters in Christ.

I THESSALONIANS was written to very new converts of Paul. **Chapters 1-2** describe their tu*in word only, but also in power and in the Holy Spirit...and you became followers of us and of the Lord* (1:5-6). Paul then speaks of his ministry among them. His team were tireless, open and honest, and like fathers to children encouraged them to walk consistently with the Lord. Paul also cites how their ministry was cut short and that **Satan hindered** their return to them.

Chapter 3 tells of their comfort when Timothy came to the team, telling of their strength in the faith and when facing affliction.

Chapters 4 concerns itself with the second coming of Jesus. In 4:13-18 Paul tells them that those who die in the Lord will not miss out of the time when the Lord returns for us. In fact the *dead in Christ will rise first and then we who are alive...will be caught up together in the clouds to meet the Lord in the air, and so will we be forever with the Lord.*

The term *caught up* has been translated into Latin for the word *rapture.* The three main rapture passages are John 14:1-3; Corinthians 15:51-54; and I Thessalonians 4:`3-18.

Chapter 5 takes a change in focus from the rapture to the day of the Lord. Paul used the Greek words *peri de, but concerning.* The Day of the Lord, as we have noted, means that God brings judgment and then brings about a new

111

program or a restoration of one. In the second coming there will be judgment as well as the Lord coming for His own in the clouds. In this chapter he promises that *God has not appointed us to wrath, but to obtain salvation by our Lord Jesus Christ* (v.9)

Bible students differ as to whether the Day of the Lord is a different phase of the Second Coming or the same time but a different result for the unbeliever.

II THESSALONIANS concerns the persecution the new Christians are facing, and a misunderstanding about the Day of the Lord. **Chapter 1** promises that the Lord will right all wrongs and punish the evildoers. We need only to rest in the *unveiling* of the *Lord Jesus Christ from heaven, with His mighty angels. In flaming fire taking vengeance on them that know not God...*(II Thessalonians 1:7-8).

Chapter 2 deals with the Day of the Lord and the rapture of believers (v.1). The Thessalonians had received misinformation that the Day of the Lord had already occurred.This had greatly upset these new Christians (v.2). Precisely what was the disturbing message was not made clear. However, II Timothy 2:18 may give good evidence of the heresy. Paul tells that two teachers have erred from the truth *saying the resurrection is past already.*

Paul takes great pains in explaining that the Day of the Lord has not occurred because there would be a great *falling away* from the faith, and the revealing of the *man of sin* (whom the Apostle John calls the *Antichrist*, I John 2:18}. This man of sin will exalt himself, and sit in the Temple, displaying himself as God. He is being restrained, but the *mystery of iniquity* is even now at work by Satan. Those who will follow the man of sin will be sent strong dillusion and be damned (II Thessalonians 2:3-12).

Chapter 3 contains a series of practical commands to live the Christian life. He warns against those who do not work, when they are able. They should not receive food from the church (v. 10). God's people should work quietly and not be *busybodies* (v. 13). Those that do not obey the Apostle's word should not have full fellowship with the church. However, he should *be admonished as a brother* until he comes to his senses.

I and II TIMOTHY and TITUS
(Pastoral Letters)

In **I Timothy** Paul instructs his colleague who is ministering in the church at Ephesus.

Chapter 1 warns of distraction of arguing over genealogies and Jewish myth. He charges Timothy to be faithful in ministry.

Chapter 2 writes of the necessity of public prayer. He then urges women to be modestly dressed. The most controversial passage is vv.

12-15. It urges that the women be silent and learn in silence, not to have a teaching ministry or authority over men. Such passages need to be read in the context of all the New Testament. Paul in I Corinthians 11:5 instructed that women dress in feminine garb, and could prophecy and pray in the public worship. The silence may have reflected the synagogue practice of debating a speaker after his address. The women were not to confront speakers, but discuss these matter with their husbands at home.

Paul also states that Even sinned by not submitting to her husband and Lord by eating from the forbidden tree in Eden. He makes the mysterious statement *she shall be saved by childbearing, if they continue in faith and in love and holiness with sobriety* (I Timothy 2:15).

Because we don't live when Paul ministered, this sentence may have been clear to his readers but not to us. One interpretation is that the priority of childbearing saves women from taking unscriptural authority and meddling, if they with these duties continue with faith, love, and sobriety.

Another interpretation is that the woman will be saved *by the childbearing* (literal Greek), referring to the actual virgin birth which brought forth the Messiah. They will be saved by this childbearing of Jesus, if they continue on with the faith (perseverance).

Chapter 3 speaks of the requirements of the bishop and deacon. The bishop (overseer) is also called an *elder,* and a *pastor* (shepherd). See Acts 20:28-29. The deacons assisted the pastors/elders possibly overseeing physical needs (Acts 6). The word *deacon* means *servant.*

Paul spends most of his instruction on maturity and Christian character. The only difference between an overseer/elder is that they must be able to teach.

Chapters 4-6 urge Timothy to remain faithful to his calling: to minister wisely to young and old, despite his youth; to be aware of false teachers; and to make sure the elders of the church are paid.

II Timothy continues to encourage Timothy to minister the truth.

Chapter 1, he must hold on to God's Word.

Chapter 2, he must teach the word.

Chapter 3, he must abide in it, knowing that falsehood will come. The Scriptures are inspired by God (literally, *God breathed)* and used by the Lord to furnish thoroughly the man of God. (3:16-17).

Chapter 4, he is to proclaim the Word of God. (Outline from Hendriksen, *New Testament Commentary).*

Titus was a Greek convert of Paul's ministry. He often had difficult assignments and is mentioned thirteen times in the New Testament.

Chapter 1 deals with the standards for overseers, similar to I Timothy.

Chapter 2 commands that Titus speak of the manner of life Christians in all circumstances should posses, due to the work of Christ's redemption and return.

Chapter 3 reaffirms the gospel that we are not saved by our own works of righteousness. Also, he must not allow those who teach heresies to have a part in the church's fellowship.

PHILEMON is a short letter by Paul to ask that this man receive his runaway slave, Onesimus. The slave has repented and come to faith in Christ. Therefore Philemon should forgive him and receive him as a brother. Here we see how Christianity undermined the very concept of slavery in the Roman empire. (See page about slavery and the Bible.)

CHAPTER FOURTEEN: THE GENERAL LETTERS: Hebrews, I, II Peter, I, II, III John, & Jude

HEBREWS deals with the superiority of the New Covenant over the Old. It is especially addressed to Hebrew Christians. The letter does not have an author's name, though he is well-known (13:18-25). The writer mentioned Timothy and ends his letter much like Paul. The early church held the letter was from Paul. While the style of writing is different, this may only be due to subject matter or a secretary, who would write in his own style under the direction of Paul.

Chapters 1-5 declare the *superiority* of Christ over *angels*, *Moses*, and the *Old Testament priesthood*. The writer points out not only is Jesus over David, but he is a *Priest after the order of Melchizidek* (Psalm 110:4; Hebrews 5:5-6). Melchizidek was priest and king of Salem. Abraham gave him tithes. So our Lord by the Sovereign will of God is a High Priest of a better covenant. The writer complains that the readers should know these things, but they have the comprehension of recent converts, because they are wasting their time arguing with those who want to follow Moses but not Christ.

Chapter 6 tells them to go on to deeper and more solid truth. He states that if one had experienced the truth of Christ and really turned away, no one could really persuade him. However, he is convinced that his readers have faith and life that *accompany salvation* (v. 9).

Chapter 7 reveals that Christ is superior to the Old Testament priesthood in that He ascends into heaven to make intercession, not in a temple on earth. He is able to *save us to the uttermost* (v. 25), because He doesn't make daily sacrifices as the Old Testament priests, but accomplished salvation by offering Himself *once* (v. 27).

Chapter 8 shows us that we are under the New Covenant. While this covenant was promised to the Northern and Southern Kingdoms, it is in effect now in the church age (vv. 6-13.

Chapters 9-10 demonstrate that the Old Covenant was only symbolic of the heavenly reality. The blood of bull and goats could not take away sin. They were only a picture of the reality of Christ. Jesus made one sacrifice and died *once for all* (9:25-28; 10:10-14).

Jesus by His death opened up a new and living way to *fellowship* with God. This call us to *draw near with a true heart in full assurance of faith* (10:22). We are to *hold fast to our profession,* to promote to one another *love* and *and good works*

Chapters 11-13 begins with the examples of faith from the Old Testament. We then are to follow this *cloud of witnesses* and *run the race set before us, looking to Jesus the founder and finisher of our faith* (12:1-2). We are encouraged to keep on enduring the disciplines the Lord brings upon our path. We belong to an unshakeable kingdom (vv. 3-39). We should be mindful of acts of kindness, hospitality, and faithfulness in marriage. We should be very mindful of our church leaders. We then are assured we will be fully equipped through the *blood of the everlasting covenant* (the new covenant).

JAMES, the Lord's brother, became a leader in the Jerusalem church. There's no mention of the council in Jerusalem (Acts 15 around A.D. 50). It may therefore be the oldest book of the New Testament.

Chapter 1 James addresses his readers as those *which are scattered abroad.* These would be the members of his congregation who were scattered to be joyful in trials, because God will bring about patience and wisdom through them. We are to be *doers of the word and not hearers only.*

Chapter 2 challenges us to be mindful of the poor who have come to faith (vv. 1-12). He then challenges one who *says he has faith.* It is invalid if it isn't accomplished by works, especially, having compassion and helping those in need (vv. 15). James is not disputing that we

119

are saved by faith **alone** (vv.23). However true faith results in action (Ephesians 2:10) *Faith without works is dead* (2:20; Also, Paul in Ephesians 2:10).

Chapters 3-4 cover practical instruction about disciplining the tongue, avoiding pride and worldliness, and relying on the Lord for business.

Chapter 5 tells the seriously sick to call the elders and be anointed by oil, as a Jewish custom. He then declares the *the prayer of faith will save the sick.* This doesn't discount means (I Timothy 5:28). When the Apostle Paul and Luke healed the people on Malta, Paul healed many miraculously (Acts 28:6) However, some were healed by Luke the physician (v.10).The word for healing by Luke is the term used for therapeutic agents (*Criswell Study Bible*).

I PETER is preparing Christians who will face localized persecution from the unstable Nero.

Chapter1, Peter reminds them of their salvation through the Trinity (1:2-11). He then tells them to live holy lives and focus on gospel truth, because *the word of the Lord endures forever* (1:24).

Chapter 2 instructs that we are livin g stones (v. 5) connected to Christ the cornerstone. We are to live and display good works before the Gentile world. We are to honor all who are in government, love our brothers in Christ, and fear God. We are to be prepared to suffer as Christ did, and to commit ourselves to God, as He did.

Chapter 3:1-11 gives practical instruction in marriage. Women are to *obey* their husbands' faith, while men are to *live with their wives according to knowledge.* (These are areas that mature Christians need to help in marriage relationships.)

Chapters 3:12-4:19 gives more instruction for living under the coming persecution.

Chapter 5 gives instruction on how an elder should feed God's flock, not focus on money, and not be a dictator (vv. 1-4). In general we are to humble ourselves to one another, casting all our care upon Him who cares for us, and resist the devil,who is like a roaring lion (vv. 5-11). Peter gives greeting from *Babylon*, which was the code-name for the city of Rome.

II PETER

Chapter 1 reminds us that they must take hold of God's promises and add to their experience greater Christian character. He also informs us that prophets wrote as they were moved by the Holy Spirit.

Chapter 2 warns against false teachers. Their end is so severe that it would have been better if they had not known the truth of Christ.

Chapter 3 speaks of the coming of Christ. He answers the *scoffers* who ask when He is coming. *One day is with the Lord as a thousand years, and a thousand years as one day* (v.8). He tells us that in participating in building Christ's kingdom is *hastening the day of God* (v. 12). Finally, he tells us that Paul's letters are also Scripture (vv.15-16).

I JOHN written by the Apostle John, who wrote the Gospel.

Chapter 1 concerns itself with our fellowship with God. John tells us of his eyewitness encounter with Jesus. Yet, he says that all of us can have a close fellowship with Jesus as well (vv. 1-4). We must walk in the light of Christ. This will expose us to our sin, but if we *confess our sins, He is faithful and just to forgive us our sins and to cleanse us from all unrighteousness* (vv. 5-10).

Chapter 2 tell us that Christ has made *propitiation* (satisfaction) for sin (v. 2).He tells us that in stages of life we are to love the brethren (vv. 3-14). However, we are not to love the world (system). This is characterized by *lust of the flesh, the lust of the eyes, and the pride of life* (v. 15). In other words satisfying desires outside of God's will and morality. We see these elements in the temptation of Eve in the Garden of Eden (Genesis 3:6). This is also observed in the Devil's temptation of our Lord (Matthew 4:3-11). He also speaks of the coming *antichrist* at the end of the age. However, he also reveals that there will be many *antichrists* before the final great one. However, all true believers have an *anointing from the Holy One* and will not be deceived by them (2:18-29).

Chapters 3-4 rehearse the same themes. We are the recipients of God's love and are *called the children of God* (3:1). Characteristic of a true believer is that he *sins not* (v. 6). However, he also says every believer deceive himself if he feels he has not sinned (1:8). What does he mean *sins not* (3:6, 8,9, 10*)? We must understand the Greek present tense conveys continuous action.* When John writes *sins not* it means he *does not continually sin.*

He then tells us that as followers of Jesus, we must give ourselves in love to one another as Jesus gave Himself to us (3:11-24). He then gives us truth how we can have *assurance of our salvation. 1) We believe that Jesus is the Christ (Messiah). 2) We love those who love Christ* (5:1-3). *3) We overcome the evil in the world,*(v. 5). *4) We are given an inner witness of the Holy Spirit that Jesus is the Son of God, and the Lord has given us eternal life, which is in the Son* (vv. 10-11).

One purpose for John's letter was for those who believe on Christ, they will know (have assurance) of possessing eternal life (v.13). This will give us confidence that the Lord will hear our prayers (v.15).

II JOHN is a short letter addressed to the *elect lady and her children.* This may mean a prominent woman in the church who won and cares for many who have come to faith. John rejoices in their faith (vv. 1-6). He warns of deceivers and antichrist teachers who have come into the world. Those who do not hold to the teachings about Christ should not be sponsored or put up in believer's homes (vv. 7-13).

III JOHN seems to be written to the same group. John calls himself the *elder* due to his great age. He rebukes Diotrephes, a man who likes the prominence in the church, (v. 10). John plans to arrive at the church and meet all face to face. We need to be aware of those who are lifted up in pride and seek to control the church for their own ends.

JUDE is a short letter that is much like Peter's writing. He warns of false teachers. He tells us that the content of our faith was **once delivered to the saints** (believers). We are not to look for new revelations or follow teachings other than what was laid down to us by the Apostles and prophets. We must be aware of false teachers and rescue those who fall for them. His benediction is a great promise of the One who will *keep us from falling* (v.24).

Chapter Fifteen:
REVELATION

REVELATION is a book with many visions and coded words. However, it promises to bring blessing to those who read and heed it (1:3). However, it also brings curses on those who take away its truths and warnings (22:18-19).

Personally, I believe most difficulty comes with *over interpreting* this book. The author John is given these visions to encourage that the Kingdom of Christ will triumph and God will bring justice. Read the book for the plain sense. We don't have to know all the meaning of every vision. However, we can receive the imagery and impact of all of them.

The basic visions given to John are divided into three parts. **Write the things you have seen, the things that are, and the things which will be hereafter** (1:19).

The past vision is of Christ (1:9-17). Jesus is visualized in His judgment. His hair is white (the ancient of days); His face like the sun; His eyes like flames of fire; His robe white, his sash around His waist, gold; out of His mouth comes a two edged sword; his feet like burnished bronze; and His voice like the roar of many waters. He stands in the midst of seven lamp-stands, which represent the seven churches, and in His hands are seven stars, which are the seven angels (or messengers) of the of judgment

The present visions are of the seven churches that existed in what is now eastern Turkey. Here seven actual churches are judged by Christ. (Judgment begins at the house of God).

, **Chapters 2-3** speak of the risen Lord's evaluation of each congregation, based on the vision of the glorified Christ, noting: *Christ's Authority, Christ's Accusations, Christ's Admonitions, and Christ's Assurances.*

Chapters 4-22. *The future visions,* **things which must be hereafter** (4:1), are recorded in these chapters They are in the main visions of judgments that will punish a wicked world and bring the nations to glorify the Lord, (5:10; 11:15; 12:5; 15:4; 19:15; 20:9,10).

Chapter 4 introduces *heaven,* where there is described God's throne, the Holy Spirit, the beings symbolizing God's rule over all creation, and the 24 elders. Since they are not angels (7:1), and have victory crowns and white robes of the redeemed, many have interpreted them to be the glorified church. Since all believers are considered priests, the number 24 might be an allusion to the 24 divisions of priests made by David for the Temple ritual.

Chapter 5 introduces the *Seven Sealed Scroll.* Only Christ can open theses seals, whose end results are the punishment of the wicked and the rule on earth of the faithful (5:10).

126

THE SIX SEAL JUDGMENTS, CHAPTER 6

1. The White Horse speaks of conquest (v.2)
2. The Red Horse speaks of war (vv. 3-4)
3. The Black Horse speaks of famine (v. 5)
4. The Pale Horse speaks of death (v.8)
5. The Martyrs speak of the need for judgment (vv. 9-11).
6. The population of the world mourns over the wrath of the Lamb (vv. 12-17).

THE INTERLUDE OF THE 144,000 AND THE MULITUDE, CHAPTER 7

The 144,000 are divided up into the twelve tribes of 12,000 each. They seem to be protected (sealed) from the judgments of the seven trumpets to come (vv. 1-8). In chapter 14:4 they are called the *first fruits for God and the Lamb.*

The other group are a *multitude who no man could number* (vv. 9-17). They are worshipping the Lord and wear white robes like the martyrs of chapter six. They are described as those who *are coming out of tribulation, the great one* (literal Greek).

The term *tribulation, the great one* could be describing what the Olivet Discourse terms *great tribulation* (Matthew 24:21), *affliction* (Mark 131:9), and *great distress* (Luke 21:23). However, the Olivet Discourse seems clearly

127

prophesying the destruction in A.D. 70. Moreover, there is evidence that Revelation was written after the destruction of Jerusalem (Revelation 17:10). *The Great Tribulation*, to our mind, is the greater intensity of future judgments that occur during the seven trumpets, seven bowls and the fall of "Babylon."

THE SEVEN TRUMPET JUDGMENTS, CHAPTERS 8-11

The seventh seal is opened and trumpets begin (8:1-5)

1. Hail, fire, and blood are cast on the earth and one third of vegetation is burned up (8:7).
2. A great mountain with fire is cast into the sea and a third of it becomes blood, and a third of sea life perishes (vv.8-9).
3. A great star called *Wormwood* falls and a third of fresh water becomes poison and a third of the population dies.
4. A third of the sun, moon and stars do not shine (v. 12)

THE THREE WOES OF THE TRUMPETS (9:12-13; 11:18)

5. A fifth angels sounds his trumpet and opens the bottomless pit. (This is the "holding place" for certain fallen angels and eventually Satan, II Peter 2:4). These demons look like locusts, have

scorpion tails, women's hair, crowns of gold, breastplates or iron, wings that sound like chariots, they inflict pain for five months (a season of growing crops). Apparently, these demons stir up a mindset for war. *This is the first woe* (9:1-11).

6. The sixth angel blows its trumpet and there comes an army of 200,000,000. They're depicted as wearing armor with brimstone, with horses like lions' heads, and tails of serpents. War result in killing one third of the human race. In today's population that would be like exterminating all of North, Central, and South America. *This is the second woe.*

NEXT INTERLUDE: THE GREAT ANGEL AND THE TWO PROPHETS, CHAPTERS 10-11

In **Chapter 10** John sees a great angel who tells him that the seventh trumpet will reveal the finishing of the *mystery of God*, which God revealed to His *prophets* (v. 7). The prophets of the Old Testament predicted the world wide triumph of Israel and all the nations worshipping the Lord. The *mystery* speaks as to how this will be done. This was not given to the Old Testament writers. However, it will be revealed in the *seventh trumpet.*

Chapter 11 begins with a command for John to measure the inner Temple, not its outer courts. This is similar to the command to Amos

7:7-8. This implies condemnation, as the worship of the Lord does not measure up. It also speaks of the time of Gentiles who trample the outer court and Jerusalem for 42 months. This is the same time given to the last half of Daniel seven years as shown in Daniel 9, 11, and 12.

The two prophets testify to the Lord. They are compared to Moses, Elijah, and Zerrubabel. They are martyred, then raised form the dead. An earthquake occurs. Seven thousand are killed and the rest give glory to God (11:1-14)

7. The Seventh Trumpet (the third woe). The announcement in v. 15 translates in the literal Greek, *the kingdom of this world becomes the Lord's and His Messiah.* The word *becomes* is the Greek aorist, which has no reference to time. We translate it in the present because the bowl judgments are in the future and the Lord is to come back fighting against the wicked and the Devil. (*Culminative Aorist,* Dana and Mantey).

THE INTERLUDE OF THE SEVEN PERSONAGES, CHAPTERS 12-14

1. **The Pregnant Woman**, clothed with the sun, a crown with 12 stars, and the moon at her feet. (12:1,2) She is Israel, not Mary, because she's chased

into the wilderness by the devil and produces children for *time, times, and a half* (meaning 3 ½ years, vv. 6,11-17).

2. **The Red Dragon**, who is the Devil, seeks to devour the coming child.

3. **The Child** is born, escapes the Devil and is caught up to heaven and will rule the earth *with a rod of iron* (v.5; 19:15; Psalm 2:9).

Why is not the cross and resurrection mentioned like Revelation 1:5? Because, Revelation 4-20 speaks of our Lord's judgment and coming rule, the results of His redemption.

4. **Michael and his angels** make war against the Dragon and throw him and his demons out of heaven. Then he begins to persecute all who belong to Jesus for the 3 ½ years (vv. 7-12).

5. **The Beast from out of the Sea** (the Antichrist, 13:1-10) is like a leopard, has feet like a bear, and a mouth like a lion, standing for Greece, Persia, and Babylon. These were the standards of the ancient foes of Israel. He has seven heads (7 kings) and ten horns with crowns, his confederates. He speaks like the Dragon and is worshipped like him

The number of the Beast (Antichrist) is 666. It is a code John gives. The letters in Hebrew of *Ceasar Nero* add up to 666. The Roman authorities wouldn't know Hebrew, but the Hebrew Christians would know it and tell their Gentile brethren. Nero was a type of the ultimate Antichrist.

6. **The Beast from the Land**, looks like a lamb but speaks like a dragon (13:11-16). He is the **false prophet** and can work miracles. He also arranges that all who buy and sell must receive a mark of loyalty to the beast (19:20).

7. **The 144,000** meet the Lord on Mount Zion after His coming. They are the firstfruits of this time of the Great Tribulation (14:1-5).

THE ANGELIC ANNOUNCEMENTS AND THE HARVEST OF WRATH

Chapter 14:6-20 brings the first announcements of three angels. 1) Fear God for the time of judgment has come (vv.6-7). 2) Babylon the Great is fallen (v.8). 3) All who bear the mark of the beast will receive eternal torment, but those *who die in the Lord will rest from their labors, their works follow them* (vv. 9-13).

> **Their Works Follow Them**
> We live not only for the Lord but to set an example for our children, grandchildren, nieces and nephews. Who knows that our lives may become a bright light to them after we pass away.

A second great harvest of earth is thrown into the winepress of God's wrath. The blood is as high as five feet and spreads for 180 miles. This is a figure of speech called an *hyperbole*, that is an understood exaggeration. It is to give us the ghastly impression of the final war of Armageddon (vv. 17-20).

THE SEVEN BOWLS OF WRATH

Chapter 16 reveals the seven bowls of wrath that are poured out at the end of the age.

1. **Painful sores** on those who worshipped the Beast and had his mark (v.2)
2. **Seas turn to blood** and all sea life dies (v.3).
3. **Rivers and springs** turn to **blood** (vv. 4-7).
4. The **Sun** causes **scorching heat** (vv. 8-9).
5. The **Beast and his kingdom** is plunged into **deep darkness** (vv. 10-11).
6. **Euphrates River dries up** permitting the kings of the east to come and form an alliance with the Beast (vv. 10-16).
7. A **Great Earthquake** splits the City of Babylon into three parts. Islands and mountains are leveled. **100 pound hailstones** fall to earth (v.17).

THE IDENTITY AND FALL OF BABYLON THE GREAT

Chapter 17 speaks of the Prostitute who sits on seven heads of the beast (13:1-10). These heads are hills (vv. 7-9) the word for mountain and hill is the same in Greek. Also the code word for Rome among the Christians was *Babylon* (I Peter 5:16).

The Prostitute carries on all kinds of *abominations* with the kings of the world. She is also *drunk with the blood of the saints and the martyrs of Jesus Christ* (v.6). She also sits on waters, which are *peoples, multitudes, nations, and tongues* (v. 15). However, the ten horns of the beast turn on the Prostitute and destroy her (v.16). These are the federation of kings linked to the Beast (Antichrist). The description of the Prostitute is reinforced by the phrase *The woman you saw is the great city which rules over the kings of the earth* (v. 18).

Chapter 18-19:15 give more detail how the city of Rome is destroyed. This causes economic and social destruction.

THE MARRIAGE SUPPER OF THE LAMB

Chapter 19:6-10 reveals the Marriage Supper of the Church to the Savior. In ancient Middle Eastern marriage ceremonies you have 1) The engagement and pledge of the dowry. To break the engagement was the height of insult

134

and rarely happened. After this legal pledge, 2) there is the coming of the groom to the house of the bride, where he and his party escort the bride into the grooms home. The bridal party then 3) celebrate the covenant with feasting (usually lasting for a week).

OUR SPIRITUAL WEDDING WITH CHRIST
1. We are pledged to Christ or engaged, waiting for His coming.
2. At His coming we are married to Christ
3. Then being ever with the Lord there is the celebration or marriage supper.

JESUS' RETURN TO EARTH

Jesus is depicted as a conqueror on a while horse. This is symbolic for conquest (6:2). Literally, He will come as He ascended (Acts 1:11). He fights with the sword from His mouth, the Word of God and judges with the ron of iron (Revelation 19:15).

Who accompany the Lord to earth? We are told they are the *armies of heaven.* II Thessalonians 1:7 tells us the Lord will be *revealed from heaven with his mighty angels.*

However, Revelation 17:14 tells us that those who come with the Lord as conquerors are the *called, chosen and the faithful.* Therefore, not only the angels but the resurrected believers will return with Jesus.

THE BINDING OF SATAN

Chapter 19:15-21 describes the warfare on of the Beast and the False Prophet. Oddly, while these two are cast into Lake of Fire, Satan is bound for a 1,000 years and put into the bottomless pit. This portion has provoked many debates about the interpretation of verses 4-10. A term for a *thousand* is the Latin *millennial.* So this 1000 years is called the *millennium.* The explanation of the positions of Bible students can become quite confusing. I'll do my best to clarify (See page 137).

Chapter 20:5 speaks of the "second resurrection" of the millennium. The Premillennial view hold that the first resurrection is literal. The Post and A millennial view holds that it is spiritual or heavenly. *However, all agree that the second is literal.*

THE WHITE THRONE JUDGMENT

A Great White Throne appears and the old earth *fled away* (20:11). Books are open and all are judged according to their works (vv. 12-14). Why is there judgment according to our works, if we cannot be saved by works? We are saved by faith that works (Ephesians 2:10; James 2:18). This is a court and evidence of grace is displayed. Moreover, millions hope they will *merit* salvation by their works. This is impossible, because *all have sinned and come short of the glory of God* (Romans 3:23). Those not found in the Book of Life are cast forever into the torment of the Lake of Fire (vv. 14-15).

THE 3 INTERPRETATIONS OF THE MILLENIUM

1. **The Premillennial View.** *Pre* refers to the second coming of Jesus. Therefore Christ returns before the millennium. This is inhabited by those who were converted during the judgments in Revelation 4-19. They are mortal and have offspring. The resurrected church rules them with Christ. The first resurrection of the millennium are those who were martyred in the Tribulation and Old Testament believers. The glories of Israel predicted in the Old Testament and New are fulfilled here. After 1000 years some of the offspring rebel, and are judged and damned with Satan.

2. **The Postmillennial View** holds that Christ comes back after the millennium. The rider on the Whitehorse in Revelation is Jesus and His power of the Gospel. The world will see most become Christians and all nations will govern by Christian principles. After that there will be a rebellion and Jesus will come again in judgment.

3. **The Amillennial View.** *A* means the millennium has no reference to the second coming. It is the rule of Jesus in heaven and in our hearts now. It is the church age. After this will come a rebellion and the Lord's return.

Chapters 21:-22:5

Keep the pictures of the symbolisms of eternity in your mind. There is the dwelling place of the redeemed like a bride. Its dwelling is a great cube of 1500 miles. It has foundations of jewels, resembling the rainbow. The light of the Lamb and the Father light the new world. The water of. life flows through it and the tree of life gives perpetual healing.

The Lake of Fire symbolizes eternal torment. We should keep in mind that damnation is like being burned alive forever.

So the believer's eternal state should be pictured as beautiful, and filled with life and intimate fellowship with our Lord's presence.

THE GREAT INVITATION
Chapter 22:6-21

Everyone **who is thirsty come. And whosoever will let him take the water of life freely** (v. 17). The water of life is the fullness of the Holy Spirit especially provided when Christ completed His sacrifice for sin (John 7:37-39). This satisfaction occurs when we begin and continue the journey of faith in Jesus as our Lord and Savior, It's tied especially to the Word of God which he gave(Colossians 3:16). May God allow this book and our attention to the Book of Books, the Bible, to saturate our hearts and lives.

A SPECIAL RESPONSE

Many simply believe about Jesus like they do about George Washington. He was the first president of the U.S.A. It is mere mental assent. *Believing about Jesus is not enough.* The faith required to be saved and reconciled to God is another matter. *We must give serious consideration to the claims of Christ.*

We must *trust Jesus Christ alone* for the pardon of our sins. Our deeds, family, religious ritual are no substitute. We must rely on Jesus Christ alone, who died on the cross to pay the penalty for sin and rose again to give us a new life.

Also, since we seek reconciliation to God through Jesus, we must be *willing to forsake our sins* and follow His will as revealed in the Bible. That's what repentance means.

A SPECIAL, SAVING RELATIONSHIP

Securing this relationship can be expressed by the following prayer:
Lord Jesus, I know I am a sinner and condemned to Hell. Right now I trust you to pardon my sins, past, present, and future. I also am willing to turn from my sins and be your follower for the rest of my life. Amen.

Whosoever will call on the name of the Lord shall be saved (Romans 10:13)

_____(signed)_____(date)

Steps to Take, if You've Put Your Trust in Christ.

1. Tell someone else you have now committed yourself to Christ.

2. You are starting on your journey with Christ. When you fail, confess your sins to the Lord and seek to turn from them. Our sins are already pardoned and we have *salvation* in Christ. However, daily confession and repentance restores *fellowship* with the Father.

3. The Christian life is not to be only *personal.* Jesus established His *church* so we may grow and serve Him with others. Find a local church which believes the Bible is God's Word and teaches it. Attend regularly, every Sunday. Get involved with a group in the church, make friends, and seek to learn and grow spiritually.

4. Read a portion from the Bible each day and pray. A good place to start is the Gospel of John. The first verses are hard to understand, but it is simply saying that Jesus existed with God the Father forever, He is God, became flesh and blood, and is received by faith in Him.

5. If I can help you in getting to a good church or answering questions, contact me: www.drrosslyon@gmail.com

Made in the USA
Charleston, SC
09 March 2013